THE SADOMASOCHISTIC
PERVERSION

THE SADOMASOCHISTIC PERVERSION

PERVERSION

THE ENTITY AND THE THEORIES

Franco De Masi

KARNAC

LONDON   NEW YORK

First published in 1999, in Italian, *La perversione sadomasochistica*
by Bollati Boringhieri Editore SRL

This English translation published in 2003 by
H. Karnac (Books) Ltd.
6 Pembroke Buildings, London NW10 6RE

Translated from Italian by Philip Slotkin, 2003
English Foreword © 2003 Eric Brenman

British Library Cataloguing in Publication Data

A C.I.P. for this book is available from the British Library

ISBN 1 85575 998 5

Edited, designed, and produced by The Studio Publishing Services Ltd,
Exeter EX4 8JN

10 9 8 7 6 5 4 3 2 1

www.karnacbooks.com

CONTENTS

FOREWORDS

Dr Eric Brenman

De Masi's book, is a detailed exploration of the sadomasochistic perversion: a dynamic, which Freud considered to be very important, a view that is also held by many contemporary Psychoanalysts.

De Masi considers that this highly important condition has not been given the study and exploration, which is warranted. He was strongly dissatisfied with the quality of the literature on this subject and what he considers as the absence of a full investigation of the deeper meaning of the perversion itself.

This book attempts to address this imbalance with a scholarly, wide-ranging and detailed study. He examines the terminology used in the analysis of sadomasochism and surveys extensively and in detail, the theories of other psychoanalysts. He further explores the relationship between sadomasochism and depression; its relationship to psychosis, borderline states, and many other conditions. He leaves very few stones unturned. He discusses the nature of evil—reparable and irreparable—in the broadest way possible. The reader has a rare opportunity to increase his/her awareness of the operation of sadomasochism in clinical practice, drawing from many diverse views, as well as those of the author.

Although writing extensively on the diversity of sadomasochism, the author attempts to establish a new theoretical basis of pure sadomasochism, in which he vigorously challenges the theories of a sexual basis of sadomasochism. He sets himself a formidable task, and states that: "Metaphysically speaking my aim is the isolation within a complex organism of a cell that I call the sadomasochistic monad in which I place the mental experience of destructive pleasure." He goes on to say that he attempts to locate a cell containing constant basic characteristics.

De Masi recognizes the complexity and difficulty of his task. In his criticism of the view of sexuality being the bedrock of sadomasochism, he even goes so far as to raise the question of the validity of an entire theory of psychoanalysis being based on sexuality. He questions the ability of researchers to penetrate what he calls "the intimate essence of sexuality". Later he says, "It is hard to identify what is natural and what is learned in human sexual behaviour." In short, he stresses the inevitable interaction which takes place, whether we like it or not, and whether we know it or not. His argument is compelling but I consider that this must apply also to his attempt to isolate the sadomasochistic monad itself.

The problem I have is to work out where De Masi stands in his evaluation of the dynamics of sadomasochism. I entirely agree with his statement in Chapter 9 where he states "I myself regard perversions in general, and the sadomasochistic perversion in particular, not as the pathological accentuation of certain infantile component drives, but as a distorted development not only of sexuality but of the entire organization of the personality and the mental structure. Sexualization as opposed to sexuality is equivalent to a special kind of mental state, an early withdrawal from reality and from relating to the world. Perversion is not a development of infantile polymorphous sexuality but a flight and withdrawal that begins in infancy through the production of sexualized mental states." If this is true, as I believe it is then the isolation of the sadomasochistic monad is a secondary consequence of the distortion of sexuality and personality, which produces the soil from which sadomasochism can flourish, isolated from human considerations.

The only other difference from my way of thinking, and perhaps the thinking of many Kleinian colleagues, is that in our view, not only is there a withdrawal from reality, but there is destruction of the perception of reality; such destruction is often exacerbated by deprivation, which in turn stimulates further destructiveness, a view which I believe De Masi does actually share. It is a view, which gives weight to the attacks on humanizing object relationships however limited these may be. The other minor point which I would like to add is that his reference to sexualized mental states (quoting from Meltzer) might be more meaningfully described as sensuous states which obliterate object relationships from awareness, in such a way as to insist that human relationships play no part. I say this because I very much applaud in his work, not the isolation of the sadomasochistic monad, but the linking of sadomasochism with the elimination of human object relationships.

At the same time I have in studying his work, come round to seeing the value of an attempt to isolate this monad. In all sciences, whether this is astronomy, biology or even theoretical physics, we both isolate a factor and study interaction. No man is an island, yet at the same time he is a unique individual. Pluralism and individuality exist side by side.

The further complication in human behaviour is that two systems also exist—the inevitable composition of our genetic primitive nature together with the powerful forces of humanization, love and concern and the awareness of the importance of what seems to be ethical, right and true—and the conflict between them which ensues. From my point of view I find this most meaningfully expressed in the constant interaction between the paranoid schizoid and depressive positions—the bedrock of Kleinian analysis. In this we require an appropriate respect for each component—a respect for the primitive, its position, its value and the realization of how impoverished we would be without these passions, and equally, the attachment to strong human values, which modify these primitive processes, is of absolute importance. The consequence of this leads to a limited resolvable task of being both full blooded with minimum violation of precious values, and the pursuit of truth without sanctimonious unreality. In this task, which is always imperfectly resolved, reparation takes place with the knowledge that a final unconflicting solution can never be achieved. I am unable to pursue a study of perversion without this backcloth.

I cannot do justice to the extensive erudite account of perversion so well presented in this book. I shall restrict myself to three main issues, which I consider to be important and invite comment. Firstly, the validity of an approximation to truth of the isolated monad. Secondly, the value and consequence of being aware of this monad, and thirdly the resolution or corruption which takes place in the conflict between naked passion and human values.

1. Although I do not believe that we can isolate this monad with total accuracy (and nor does De Masi in the later chapters of his book), the operation of this propensity is clearly observable. The pleasure of destructiveness albeit with different levels of intensity, is ubiquitously present—for example the attraction of victorious football teams and other competitive sports etc. are universal operations, which ordinarily are practised within limits imposed by human values. As with humour, which Freud linked with sadism.

It is generally agreed that the excess of pleasure in human destructiveness may be in inverse proportion to the weakness of love of human commitment as a concomitant. It does not seem enough to say that the pleasures of triumph in beating the opposition would not occur if there were full human development. Not to enjoy some competitive rivalry (which may even be holier than thou) would be an artefact. We would have to abandon our belief in the Oedipus complex if this were so. For me the evidence for the operation of this monad is ubiquitous. Those who are ardent fundamentalists and who believe in absolute purity do enough damage to those who do not agree with them! Those who postulate that pleasure in triumph would not take place if absolute purity were to be achieved are like those analysts who believe that one can totally eliminate problems instead of the analysis strengthening the self to cope and enjoy dealing with the vicissitudes of life—a claim which Freud put paid to in Analysis Terminable and Interminable.

2. The main thrust of psychoanalysis is the task of getting to know ourselves, where we learn that we are in some ways much worse, and in some ways much better than we think we are. What is particularly germane to this book is knowing about our sadistic pleasure in triumph and destruction that in some way makes us more alive, and in other ways can be the death of so much as well.

In Greek tragedy, the source and inspiration of much psychoanalytic exploration, this matter is so aptly addressed in the Bachae, Euripides last play, written when he was more than 80 years old, Euripides deals with the advent of the appearance of the God,

Dionysus, the god of lust, wine, triumph and destructive pleasure, who declares that he must be acknowledged as a god, demands to be worshipped and claims "You ignore me at your peril". The arrogant King of Thebes, disregards him, with frightful consequences. Disastrous consequences also result in those who indulge in the Bacchanalian orgy; those carried away in uncritical indulgence. The two wise persons, who escape this fate, are Cadmus and Thierisus, who acknowledge the Bacchanalian rite, and retain their wisdom and understanding, and have their feet firmly planted on the ground. The moral is quite clear that we both need to know (+K) and value and deal with our primitive drives and to keep alive our belief in goodness. The philosopher, Nietzsche, in his celebrated writing on the birth of tragedy, argued that tragedy was born out of the primitive source of base human instincts, uninhibited and expressed in Dionysean rituals. As we know he became taken over by these ideas and danced naked in Pagan jubilation and never recovered his sanity. It seems that he brilliantly reached contact with the primitive but lacked a container/helpmate, which could help him through to regain his sanity.

3. This cautionary tale is all important clinically—to expose oneself to these primitive destructive forces one must have ones feet firmly planted in another truth, namely the power and strength of human relationships and understanding, and not have ones feet firmly planted in the clouds, or planted in the belief that the discovery of data and theory alone is sufficient to cope with the powerful vicissitudes of life. To this thought I would like to give Freud the last word with his references to having the strength to meet the contingencies of life. In his seminal paper, Mourning and Melancholia, he cites the difference between mourning and melancholia, when he describes the mourner as going through all sorts of destructive madness, but coming through in the end because the mourner keeps alive (with the help of others) the good object which is lost in the external world but is introjected and forms part of the resources which heal and overcome destructive madness. In contrast in melancholia (really manic depression) the subject does not know what he has lost, and only has omnipotence, destructiveness available "to keep him warm".

It is clearly implied by Freud that whether the outcome is to be the successful working through of mourning, or melancholia (manic/depression), depends upon the access to valued good loving experience or not. This in turn depends upon whether the person in question knows that such a humanizing object is needed.

Applying this understanding to De Masi's account of sadomasochistic practice could be useful. De Masi writes: "In sadomasochism by contrast to ordinary sexuality which is bilateral, only one protagonist must experience all the pleasure; the more the sadist's partner has no pleasure or experiences unpleasure, the more satisfied he is. The sadist is aroused by domination and the masochist by submission." De Masi states that he introduces the sadomasochistic monad to describe the fusional fantasy of one party having all the experiences and the other identifying with the sadist. It does seem to me that one party has all the meaning and the other is of no significance.

The monad (ultimate unity, the deity) is not in life a thing in itself, which totally generates all fulfilments. This monad does not have intercourse in the give and take sense and there is no cross fertilization and subsequent creativity. Indeed whatever the claims of the sadist may be in having it all and being it all he needs another to validate the corruption that he the sadist is everything and entitled to be supplied with everything: a corruption that concomitantly asserts that the masochist is worthless and contributes nothing and who only becomes worthwhile by identifying with the sadist.

The pervert, perverts the truth and the course of justice. He steals the love of the other whose judgement is perverted to believe that the cruel manic triumph is far superior to the human creative intercourse; it is this creative intercourse which achieves mutual appreciation. In clinical practice the analyst is the target of the pervert's propaganda and is designated the role of giving up the analysts belief and worshipping the false monad/God.

This power cannot be over estimated. It occupies the role of the harsh superego, sometimes called the super superego. In this case the judgement of the superego is to demand unconditional surrender to this edict and the depressed person is not helped to repair damage but to declare his worthlessness and unfitness to live.

No one completely escapes this, and I agree with De Masi who I understand considers that no one is without this pleasure in destruction. It is knowing this and realistically valuing the achievement of loving intercourse, which modifies this corrupting monad.

Still giving Freud the last word, I want to link this with De Masi's work on the corruption of the truth. In favourable circumstances, the struggle between love and hate, good and bad, may hopefully result in the good gaining ascendancy. The consequence is guilt, partial reparation, mourning and rebuilding. The task, which we all have to face, is coping with the corruption. De Masi implies that a corruption takes place under the flag of sexuality which has creation and loving implications, but this becomes corrupted in sensual delight which harnesses the omnipotent destruction, where the sadist appropriates all significance and denies meaning in the other.

This book covers such a wide range, which provokes creative thinking, an essential feature that enables us to explore the power of sadomasochism, with the recognition of the need for and efficacy of creative endeavour. It is a truly revealing study, which is a considerable contribution to the understanding of the omnipresent factor of sadomasochism.

Dr Eric Brenman,
former President of British Psychoanalytical Society.

Francesco Barale

"Hate, as a relation to objects, is older than love"

Freud, 1915c, p. 139

"Dell'Amor più desto è l'odio
le sue vittime a colpir,
[Hate is quicker than love
to strike down its victims,]

Somma, libretto of Verdi's opera *Un ballo in maschera*,
Act 1, Scene 1 (aria: "Alla vita che t'arride ...")

"Nothing happened to me, Officer Starling. *I* happened. You can't reduce me to a set of influences. You've given up good and evil for behaviorism, Officer Starling. You've got everybody in moral dignity pants—nothing is ever anybody's fault. Look at me, Officer Starling. Can you stand to say I'm evil? Am I evil, Officer Starling?"
"I think you've been destructive. For me it's the same thing." "Evil's just destructive? Then *storms* are evil, if it's that simple [...]."

Harris, 1988, p. 16

Hate—the hate of the first two of the above quotations—is indeed very far from the sadomasochism of Franco De Masi's study, one of whose many theses is that hate, a strong feeling directed towards an object, does *not* lie at the root of the sadomasochistic perversion, and is not even a component of it.

It is not hate that fuels sadistic destructiveness.

To the true perverse sadist, absolutely nothing matters about his victim as such—except, precisely, that he should be nullified and a victim. The true sadist does not hate that victim nor, through him and in his stead, and by some mysterious transference or false connection, does he hate any other more or less primal object.

In this respect (apart from the importance of "trauma", which is admittedly recognized but in no way held to be "fundamental"), Dr De Masi's thought diverges radically from other prominent contemporary theories; for example, those of an author such as Stoller (who sees perversion as the "erotic form of hatred"), to which they bear some (but not many) resemblances.

However, sadomasochism involves still less the passions of melodrama—let alone those of Verdi's plots—which are replete not only with hate but also with love, jealousy, power, longing, and the like.

Indeed, what is perhaps even more unexpected—at least to a reader unfamiliar with Franco De Masi's tenacious exploration of the perverse dimension, which has extended over many years—is that, in his view, neither love nor sex seems to have anything to do with it. Any theatre of the passions, be they "red" or "black", already lies, in his view, outside the boundaries of the perverse scene proper.

Dr De Masi's theory of the sexual perversions, or at least of the sadomasochistic perversion, is paradoxically not sexual, not erotic and, I would say, not object-related.

The innovation here, although one might be inclined to believe otherwise, does not lie in his placing the roots of sadomasochism outside the realm of sexuality. That is in fact an old idea: from the beginnings of psychoanalysis, when the first edition of Freud's *Three Essays on the Theory of Sexuality* was published in 1905, the problem of destructiveness, cruelty and hate (and the associated problem of sadomasochism) had seemed to Freud to be metapsychologically non-reducible to that of sexuality.

Freud never solved the problem of sadomasochism within the *Sexualtheorie*, even before the turning point of 1920–1924: "love and hate [...] do not after all stand in any simple relation to each other. They did not arise from the cleavage of any common entity, but sprang from different sources, and had each its own development" (Freud, 1915c, p. 138).

The excess of infantile cruelty and sadistic destructiveness in relation to sexuality gave rise to a number of different notions and conceptualizations in the development of Freud's thought.

This is not the place to review these changes of perspective. As it happens, Dr De Masi alludes to them himself in his study, emphasizing in particular the major turning point of 1920–1924 (*Beyond the Pleasure Principle* and "The economic problem of masochism")—that is, the central position that Freud gradually came to assign to the death drive when he found himself unable to derive these phenomena from any "psychological" source. However, he also contends that this turning point is not reflected in the subsequent literature, apart from a few Kleinian and post-Kleinian developments. The specificity of Franco De Masi's theory lies rather in his radical separation of sadistic destructiveness from the development of psychosexuality (and of the relational world).

In the Freudian vision, sadistic destructiveness, which is not reducible to psychosexuality (and to the construction of the world of relationships, of which psychosexual development is the matrix), is in itself essentially "silent". It is expressed through "numerous links" with sexuality, which it places in its service (although the converse is also the case); it is therefore found mixed with sexuality in infinitely varying proportions, contributes to the characterization of the various libidinal phases, and plays an important part in the construction of the relational world and its vicissitudes. Mixed with sexuality, it becomes a fundamental ingredient of mental life, of the intersubjective dimension and of fantasy.

In the vicissitudes of object cathexis, in the form of "appropriation" and domination of the object, it paradoxically contributes to the possibility of binding excitation and working through trauma. In metapsychological terms, this constitutes the link with the later "relational" and traumatic theories of sadomasochism (what Dr De Masi calls the "second paradigm" adduced to explain the sadomasochistic perversion, the first being the *Sexualtheorie*). This link has indeed been neglected, since the "relational" theories have largely abandoned the drive-based and economic standpoint (as well as metapsychology).

By instead presenting a radically non-erotic theory of perversion, Dr De Masi proceeds backwards along Freud's route, as it were undoing his progress step by step. The sadomasochistic perversion is unequivocally detached from the background of Freud's *Sexualtheorie* (and indeed also from the "development of the libido" as described by Abraham (1916), who attributed such importance to the sadistic, anal, and oral dimensions and to ambivalence towards objects; Franco De Masi is, as it happens, an eager student of Abraham).

In fact, Dr De Masi points out that the explanatory basis of the *Sexualtheorie*, from Freud's *Three Essays on the Theory of Sexuality* right down to its most up-to-date versions, is misleading: precisely the thesis of the fusion of the drives has facilitated the adoption of "continuist" and "minimalist" positions on perversion, thereby making it possible to avoid a serious theoretical and clinical confrontation with the problems posed by perverse destructiveness as an entity fundamentally antagonistic to sexuality and object cathexis.

That is no small matter. After all, the *Sexualtheorie* is the background against which psychoanalytic consideration of the perverse dimension arose and developed, under the banner of the discovery of a continuity between the vicissitudes of psychosexuality—the neuroses and the perversions—and of the realization that the roots of our mental life lie in the experience of pleasure and that the perverse nucleus is omnipresent in human sexuality (which, by its very nature, takes the form of an excess or discrepancy, "something over and above" the pure biological function).

A climate replete with humours and passions is thus not discernible in Dr De Masi's descriptions of the universe of the sadomasochistic perversion. There is no mixture of libido and destrudo; no human dialectic of life and death, of objects that are controlled or manipulated or hated or attacked or faecalized or even destroyed because they are also loved and necessary; no primal scene, no dominating but impossible Oedipus complex; no regression or fixation to ambivalent positions; and no contiguity between "normal" and "perverse" sexuality. The tragedy does not, as in the well known line from Verdi's opera *Un ballo in maschera*, turn into comedy.

Dr De Masi often cites the dissolute world of the Marquis de Sade and the later perverse contract of Sacher-Masoch as literary examples (but perhaps, with regard to the pleasure of the pure, cold domination of others, the pleasure of the destructive sexualized triumph over relationality, dependence and love—a very important theme in his theory—he could also have mentioned Choderlos de Laclos's extraordinary *Dangerous Acquaintances*). Here, though, we are if anything in the world of Dürrenmatt's *Durcheinandertal*—the "valley of chaos" pervaded by a primary, irremediable destructiveness that lies just beneath the apparent order of things.

Franco De Masi's research thus possesses an originality that distinguishes it from the psychoanalytic tradition in general and from the work of the Italian analysts who have delved into perversion in recent decades. In his view, the assumption of any continuity between sadomasochistically tinged relationships and actual sadomasochistic perversion is confusing. The confusion results precisely from the "continuist" and "minimalist" attitude, and conceals the difficulty of confronting the destructive essence of the sadomasochistic perversion proper.

However, acceptance of this discontinuity would force us to embrace the difficult task of questioning many of the *idées reçues* of psychoanalysis. Dr De Masi's voice certainly stands out from the chorus and deserves a hearing.

The theoretical and clinical implications are far-reaching. If the sadomasochistic perversion is deemed radically different in its essence, origin, development and consequences from sexuality and from the construction of the world of objects (and indeed radically opposed to them), then it cannot be held to possess any significance in terms of development from prior phases or positions, or of regression when the onward path is blocked, or of a defensive anchorage against the slide into something worse.

From this point of view, no legitimacy can be accorded to a statement such as the following (by Ismond Rosen), which Dr De Masi cites as an example of the "minimalist" mistakes resulting from the theory of the "mixture" of libido and destrudo and of the mitigation of cruelty by sexuality (as well as from the confusion between "aggression" and "destructiveness"): "Danger occurs when the perversion fails, that is to say there is insufficient libido to contain the aggression" (Rosen, 1979b, p. 54). Yet I am sure that many psychoanalysts still subscribe to this view!

In short, the sadomasochistic perversion does not concern Eros, even indirectly or in the complicated vicissitudes of its mixture with Thanatos; it does not concern the progressive or regressive movements involved in the construction of the object (whether that construction be ambivalent, steeped in aggression, or demanding control). It has nothing to do with the development of psychosexuality; it does not arise out of stumbling-blocks in its path or its component elements, and it is not in any way connected with infantile sexual polymorphism.

The sadomasochistic perversion is pure Thanatos, and comes into being in an utterly different place. It is born of a primary destructiveness, fuelled and reinforced in some cases, but not necessarily, by a wide variety of experiential and object-related vicissitudes (although not dependent on them), and tends to assume the form of—to paraphrase Meltzer—sexualized states of mind.

Note that I say "sexualized" and not "sexual" states, because sexualization has nothing to do with sexuality and with the (part or whole) objects cathected by it; although it makes use of sexuality and colonizes it, it is merely the fuel that ignites the destructive mental state.

The concept of sexualization is very important in Franco De Masi's thought. Totally in the service of primary destructiveness, sexualization is the activation of an excited, drugged mental state that permits a non-object-related and purely destructive orgasmic pleasure, which is sought for its own sake. This pleasure, which is ecstatic and "over-sensual" (übersinnlich, as Mephistopheles says to Faust; Sacher-Masoch borrows the word later), is based on the distortion of sensory perception, relationality and the human world within which Eros can be implanted; it is in fact a technique for the perverse annihilation of relationality and of Eros. It is therefore a thoroughly pathological phenomenon, which cannot be seen in terms of defence or conflict; it is often organized at an early stage on the basis of mental states of excited, destructive withdrawal, and progressively captures the minds of children who are particularly delicate, excitable or liable to excessive persecutory anxieties.

That is the primal nucleus and genesis of the perverse structure.

It is an intrinsically non-object-related and deadly nucleus, and thus constitutes not a "sexual state of mind" but a destructive one.

Dr De Masi's debt in this connection to Kleinian and in particular post-Kleinian thought and theories (mainly to Rosenfeld and Meltzer, but also to Joseph and Brenman) is manifest, acknowledged and declared, but he radicalizes these authors' ideas still further.

The result is the opposite of Freud's: whereas Freud saw perversion in continuity with "normal" development and its conflicts, anxieties and vicissitudes (whether positive or negative), thereby, if you will, "depathologizing" it as an intrinsic possibility and irremediable nucleus of the human condition, Dr De Masi *pathologizes* it as the expression of a destructive nucleus by no means in continuity either with the vicissitudes of psychosexual development and relationality or with the "normal" organization of mental life. It emerges, in effect, as pure evil.

In line with this "discontinuistic" vision of the sadomasochistic perversion, and taking issue with much of the relevant psycho-analytic literature (including, recently, Kernberg, 1995), Dr De Masi denies any continuity between "normal" and "perverse" sexuality. Instead, he emphasizes the substantial clinical difference between the sadomasochistic perversion "proper" (perversion as "structure") and the variegated field of perverse acting out, of more or less episodic and defensive or compulsive perverse behaviour, or perverse manifestations symptomatic of depressive states or under-lying dissolution anxieties (as often encountered in borderline pathologies)—or between the sadomasochistic perversion and the more or less sadomasochistic dynamics of hate, aggression and control of objects that appear in a complex range of relational scenarios or clinical situations (for example, typically in melancholia).

This distinction is central to Franco De Masi's theory, but I do not think it can always be drawn easily, especially in the clinical situation. Yet his arguments in support of it deserve consideration and discussion, and some of his most interesting chapters are based on them. The chapters on areas of clinical contiguity with the sadomasochistic perversion, even where already recognized, are equally important.

A clear-cut conclusion is reached: "It is one thing to speak of sadomasochistic interpersonal dynamics, but another to draw analogies with sexual perversion. The assertion that the pervert tends to entertain personal relationships in line with his sexual disturbance does not correspond to reality. On the contrary, someone—for example, the melancholic—who constantly creates sadomasochistic relationships keeps himself well away from the world of sexual perversion [...]. It is in my view very important to describe the (object-related) interpersonal dynamics that character-ize sadomasochistic relationships and to distinguish them from the specific elements of sexual perversion proper. An extensive body of psychoanalytic literature following on from Freud and Abraham has attempted to show that sexual perversions are the outcome of conflicts between different psychical agencies (the ego and superego in particular). [...]. Pure sexual perversion does not stem from conflicts, but is actually characterized by agreement and syntony between the various parts of the self".

It follows from this basic approach that what Dr De Masi calls the second major psychoanalytic paradigm for the understanding of the sadomasochistic perversion is also insufficient, precisely because it uses wide-ranging, all-purpose concepts and catch-all clinical categories.

This paradigm denotes the general school (covered by the convenient generic adjective "relational") in which a number of tendencies converge; although these sometimes differ in major as well as minor respects, they have all contributed to the idea that perversion not only performs a defensive function in relation, for example, to psychotic anxieties (a very old thesis, to be found, for instance, in the contributions of Glover or Bergler in the 1930s), but is also a specific, more or less desperate and more or less obligatory, strategy for the restoration or preservation of the self, which develops in the absence of alternatives or in extreme situations.

The protagonists of this view include, for example, Winnicott, Khan and other authors inspired by Winnicott, and Kohut, Goldberg, Stolorow and other Kohut-inspired authors; however, similar ideas are also widespread outside these two major schools and have been espoused by many other European and American authors (e.g. Joyce McDougall in Europe and Stephen Mitchell in the USA).

The contiguity with the theme of trauma is particularly obvious here. Moreover, these ideas and theses result from the many suggestions that have accrued from the renewed interest shown during the last few decades, especially in America, in the psychic consequences of early infantile traumas or of sexual and other abuse.

In broad outline, these authors see perversion—"neosexuality" and the like—as having the function of avoiding or somehow resolving painful and intolerable mental states and affects; these manifestations reveal the existence of a self that has been violated or abused or insufficiently protected, fed and sustained—a self whose radical wounds give rise, through various, complex mechanisms, to the perverse strategy or destructive dynamic as a desperate attempt at self-care and object-relatedness.

For Stoller too, as it happens, although his vision is unique among modern theories of perversion, the link between sexuality and hate is in the service of a revenge that transforms the past experience of trauma into a present triumph.

The phenomenon of "sexualization", which is central to Dr De Masi's theory, is seen in this theoretical context as the expression of an attempt at self-reparation, as recently stated by Goldberg (1997) in the panel on perversion at the 40th IPA Congress in Barcelona.

Franco De Masi sees some merit in this school, whose protagonists, against the general background of the "crisis" of psychoanalysis, have recently been enjoying a vogue among psychoanalysts, partly because of their simplicity and the "facility" with which they short-circuit complex problems by presenting socially acceptable notions. Even so, as regards the relationalist and traumaticist approach too, Dr De Masi insists on the need for discrimination and clarity, and stresses that different phenomena must not be confused through the use of sweeping, all-purpose notions.

His objections to this basic approach to the problem of perversion fall into two groups, which are clinical and theoretical respectively.

The clinical objections centre on the consideration that, whereas the relationalist and traumaticist paradigm may throw light on some other clinical situations, this is not the case with the sadomasochistic perversion: there is no doubt that many disorders, certain episodic perversions and some pathologies characterized by problems of aggression or antisocial behaviour are directly connected with very early narcissistic wounds. However, all this has nothing (or virtually nothing) to do with the perverse structure proper, for not only is there no evidence of a correlation between early wounds or a deficiency of primal narcissistic attunement on the one hand and perversions on the other, but a great deal of clinical experience suggests the opposite. For that matter, non-psychoanalytic research, too, does not in any way bear out the hypothesis of such a correlation (in so far as this is amenable to investigation by non-psychoanalytic instruments).

Furthermore, Franco De Masi asserts that anxiety plays no part in true structured perversions. The theoretical objections revolve in particular around the argument that, whereas there are no serious grounds for assuming that a wound affecting the cohesion of the self must give rise, precisely, to the development of perverse sexuality (for if sexuality in general intrinsically performs a cohesive function, why should perversion ensue?), there are many reasons, both theoretical and clinical, for postulating a contrary relationship between fragility of the self and perversion. It is the progressive inroads made by a perverse–destructive–excited area that gradually wear down the ego (and the self): "I find it hard to see perversion as a defence against anxiety which has a restructuring function, however temporary [...]; it is surely more likely that the perverse mental state contributes to the progressive destructuring of the ego, sapping its vitality through the addictive dependence on sexual pleasure".

The relationship between trauma and perversion, too, appears highly complex and anything but linear; apart from the well-known problems raised by the concept of trauma in psychoanalysis, it is also the case that often "the trauma–perversion sequence may be reversed: in children secretly given to sadomasochistic pleasure, traumatic experiences may stimulate sexualization. In these cases trauma, rather than being seen as a source of anxiety, may rekindle the sadistic pleasure and mobilize the masochistic fantasy".

It may be wondered why Dr De Masi does not consider a third hypothesis on the relation between a wounded self and perversion—that is, the possibility that fragility of the self (and/or a particular vulnerability to trauma) and the tendency to develop perversions might be two aspects of a single basic structure, which is only partially (even if usefully) amenable to psychoanalytic investigation. At any rate, Dr De Masi concludes that it is an improbable oversimplification to regard perversion merely as a response to pain.

If I may for a moment abandon my neutral position as the writer of a foreword and express my own opinion on this point as a student of psychiatric phenomena as well as a psychoanalyst, I would say that Dr De Masi is surely right, at least on the theoretical level. Merely to substitute "wounded self" for "psychosexuality" to explain perversion is a simplification that tells us little about the specific mechanisms and nature of perversion.

Furthermore, in the panel referred to above, Goldberg, too, accepts this to some extent, in pointing to the presence of a radical split in the pervert's personality and adducing the complexity of specific individual dynamics to account for what may indeed stem from ancient wounds.

An even more radical position on this point was adopted in the same discussion by Chasseguet-Smirgel (whose views have certain features in common with De Masi's), when she noted that the idea of sexualization as an instrument for treating narcissistic wounds cannot by any means account for the production of sexual perversion. She sees sexualization as a manic operation tantamount to an attack on the mind and on relationships (in the sense of Bion's "–K"), directed towards the radical disavowal of differences, of the Oedipal links between experience and sexuality, with the aim of producing an idealized world of "anal confusion".

At clinical level it is certainly true in general that no linear relationship can be seriously assumed between hypothetical or real fundamental narcissistic deficiencies and perverse pathology. Something more, or different, is at work here.

Dr De Masi refers to the large number of stories and recorded cases in which brutal and criminal sadism has arisen out of seemingly "normal" infantile personal vicissitudes and care experiences. These cases are at least as numerous as those—which are surely more reassuring for theory—in which, more or less retrospectively (it is very easy to find what one is expecting in the retrospective dimension), the elements of a primal wound to the self can be discovered (or, at least, manifestations that can be regarded as "reactions" to some "trauma", which may perhaps be to a greater or lesser extent cumulative or continuous).

In general, among other things, psychoanalysts would do well to ponder over the bias represented by the potentially powerful direct or indirect self-confirmatory effect of their theories on clinical material and its organization and reorganization, and to consider the disastrous past and present effects of an ingenuous idea of psychogenesis on those working in the "psychosocial" field. Furthermore, of course, they must also subject their generalizations and postulated correlations to "external" validation and verification. But that is a horse of a different colour.

Personally, I could adduce many case histories in support of Franco De Masi's thesis. However, this would further extend the subject-matter of this book.

Anyone with ample psychiatric experience of working with severely ill patients, if he is not inclined towards ideological solutions and has no need of doctrinaire confirmation, will in general share Dr De Masi's puzzlement at the traumatic–relational simplifications with regard to the sadomasochistic perversion. The matter is further complicated if one is familiar with the non-psychoanalytic literature.

One of the most fruitful aspects of this study, which offers no easy alternatives, in my view lies precisely in the critique of these simplifications. In the words of Hannibal the Cannibal, the terrible criminal psychiatrist of *The Silence of the Lambs* (who knows all about sadists), let us try not to put everybody in "moral dignity pants"— not to reduce everything "to a set of influences" (Harris, 1988).

Alternatively—to remain in the scientific field—Green (1988) was right to point out some years ago that an incomprehensible gulf mostly persists between, on the one hand, life stories as we succeed in reconstructing them retrospectively or simply in hypothesizing them in our analytical consulting rooms—the internal stories which we (always retrospectively) feel to have come into being on the basis of those life stories—and, on the other, the psychopathological experiences that a given patient, with those particular (and hypothetical) stories, has developed. Green here uses, precisely, Jaspers's term "incomprehensible".

I am not at all convinced that, as Green appears to suggest, in the absence of anything else, all we can do is to try to bridge this gulf with psychoanalytic aetiological myths; if one is not inclined to put "dignity pants"—this time theoretical or mythological ones—on to the world, that gulf often remains enigmatic, and gives rise to more questions than answers. I say this with all due respect to myth, both old and new (and its relationship with enigma). Moreover, that gulf is the original field of study of classical psychopathology, which has perhaps been dismissed with excessive haste.

Yet all this surely applies not only to the sadomasochistic perversion, but in fact to more or less all situations of severe psychopathology. All serious evidence in the field of contemporary psychopathological and psychiatric research strongly suggests that psychopathological phenomena are highly complex and that directly traumatic or ingenuously psychogenetic hypotheses are untenable.

There is something more and something different.

As to the sadomasochistic perversion, Dr De Masi here presents his rigorously psychoanalytic attempt to account for this "something different", which he sees as a colonization and progressive invasion by destructive, excited areas of the mind—areas that develop, not continuously with and in a manner derivable from normal sexuality and relationality (including all the phenomena of ambivalence and the complicated feelings and positions as classically described), but in ways that impair and distort these.

Through his attempt, Franco De Masi bravely poses for psychoanalytic consideration a number of questions with far-reaching implications. A general lesson can be drawn from his radical theses, whether or not they are shared and whatever one's views on the sadomasochistic perversion (on which I, for one, am certainly more attached than he to the classical notion of the fusion of drives).

As stated at the beginning of this foreword, Dr De Masi considers that if the full implications of the destructiveness involved in the sadomasochistic perversion and its non-derivability from psychosexual development are accepted, many commonplaces, mythologies, and stereotypes of psychoanalysis will logically be called into question.

A particularly important example of these current mythologies is considered briefly towards the end of this book, and in my opinion deserves to have been developed differently. It concerns the idea of a "continuum" linking the "primitive" and the "pathological".

Dr De Masi notes that Caper (1988) recently published some

interesting observations on this notion, which he attributes to the fact that psychopathological states contain the idealization, concreteness, fantastic anxieties and grandiosity that are also found in normal infantile mental states. This coincidence wrongly suggests that pathology is a pure concretization of primitive mental states. Such an explanation is reassuring but false. The forces at work in the perversions and in psychopathological states are destructive ones that progressively destroy the capacities on which mental health depends, which include the functional dependence on human objects and the possibility of learning from emotional experience.

The equating of "pathological" and "primitive" in psychopathology is an illusion similar in every respect to the now obsolete one that underlay the old anthropological equation of "psychotic" with "primitive".

The problem can be restated in these terms: anything, whatever its source, that appears in or bursts into mental experience is bound ultimately to assume meaning and to form part of the overall vicissitudes of the individual human life concerned (and will do so in a manner to a greater or lesser degree integrated, constructive or destructive). But this tells us nothing about its origin.

The "continuist" mythologies and the consequent representations and stereotypes of development (not only in relation to pathology) were discussed some years ago in an illuminating book by Jerome Kagan (1986) *The Nature of the Child*, which had only a somewhat embarrassed review in the *International Journal of Psycho-Analysis*.

However, let us not digress further from Dr De Masi's subject. It may indeed be wondered whether his disquisition on the origins of perverse destructiveness does not at the same time take us to the very heart of our discipline and to its limits.

Let me conclude my notes on this book, which is the fruit of genuine thought and the courage to stand out from the crowd, with a comment that may seem rather "minimalist".

While Dr De Masi's radical position compels us to engage in salutary exercises of detachment from established psychoanalytic ideas and to abandon any sanitized image of perversion, it may perhaps be at risk of suggesting a dichotomized conception and hence the idea of the irremediability of evil.

The final pages of the study, on therapy, are important in this connection. With clinical wisdom, Dr De Masi tackles the subject in terms of the position occupied by the perverse experience and structure in the overall context of the personality. This, however, is already a way of placing perversion within a continuum. To be sure, the actual perverse experience (like the psychotic experience) is not analysable as such. It is at most a matter, where possible, of working "on the context", to make it less devastating. Again, as is well known and as Dr De Masi points out, the true pervert will not request psychoanalytic therapy.

Then there is the problem of the countertransference in response to severe perverse manifestations. Whereas any genuine process of psychoanalytic elaboration necessarily entails identification and sharing, what happens when the analyst is confronted with accounts of experiences of mental states that seem so "alien" or repugnant to him?

But perhaps I am too attached to the old idea of the fusion of the various drive currents to be able to think in "pure" terms. Yet it is my impression that clinical work never presents us with "pure" situations, but always, precisely, with complicated mixtures in which, even in the most serious cases, the destructive aspects appear in a complex interplay of projections, splits, erotizations, defences, conflicts, and so on. In every case, these "pure" experiences ultimately mix in with the overall vicissitudes of the person's life.

The twentieth century's literary exemplar of nihilism (and anal destructiveness), Céline's *Journey to the End of Night*, is thoroughly pervaded, below the surface, by an intense longing for an impossible tenderness and object-relatedness, which shines through at times (the exchange with Molly, the child's death which Ferdinand cannot prevent, etc.). However, much of the book's fascination lies precisely in the desperate tension of this longing.

At the end of *Dangerous Acquaintances*, Valmont falls in love and the Marquise de Merteuil is tormented with jealousy: the perverse heroes of the cold dominion over the other discover the misfortunes of object-relatedness. Is this a "decent", hypocritical ending, as Malraux maintained?

It is not always the case that the terror in the victim's eyes excites the sadist and goads him on to perform the criminal act of homicide, as with the serial killer mentioned by Dr De Masi. In one profoundly sadistic subject observed by me, it was precisely this mutual eye contact, the flash of infinite terror in the victim's eyes, that for a moment allowed the split to be overcome and opened the way to an identification with his own terrified, mortified, sadistically attacked aspects—those involved in his constant and severe destructive perverse acting out—thus affording a tiny, precarious contact with good, affectionate objects ... Am I here trying to sugar the pill of Franco De Masi's thesis?

By no means. Anyone familiar with the perverse experience and in particular with the sadomasochistic perversion cannot but share Dr De Masi's fundamental pessimism in regard to its capacity to dominate the mind and its inaccessibility to relationality. Yet it is not a monolithic entity but a complex experience, with an internal dynamic and internal contradictions; at times it is, or may appear, completely split off from the overall libidinal side of human life, which it may seriously colonize, whereas on other occasions it preserves many "links" with that side.

So, precisely for this reason, given all the sacrosanct pessimism of intelligence, all the Freudian consciousness that the "big battalions" are in the enemy camp, all the experience that shows how far the splits and disavowal governing the perverse organiza- tion are irreducible to any analysis and prevent vital, mutative exchanges, and all our awareness of the enormous importance and irreplaceability of perverse acting out in the overall libidinal economy (perverse pleasure, when it becomes established, becomes a powerful "attractor" to which no other pleasure can compare)— given all these caveats, it may nevertheless be possible to keep a door open to hope. This book's insistence on clarity and its invitation to delve more deeply and more radically into the phenomenon open the way to a positive approach based on the intuition that, if we know the "enemy camp", we shall be in a better position to work in the interests of our patients.

CHAPTER ONE

Introduction

"In Diderot's tale, the good genie Cucufa discovers at the
bottom of his pocket, in the midst of worthless things—
consecrated seeds, little pagodas made of lead, and moldy
sugar-coated pills—the tiny silver ring whose stone, when
turned, makes the sexes one encounters speak. He gives it to
the curious sultan. Our problem is to know what marvelous
ring confers a similar power on us, and on which master's
finger it has been placed; what game of power it makes
possible or presupposes, and how it is that each one of us has
become a sort of attentive and imprudent sultan with respect
to his own sex and that of others"

Foucault, 1976, p. 79

This book arose principally out of the acute dissatisfaction I
felt when, wishing to investigate in depth the nature and
significance of the various forms of perversion observed in
the material or fantasies of many analysands, both male and female,
I attempted to compare my own views with the available psychoanalytic literature. I was surprised to find that there is no single,
clear-cut psychoanalytic position on this subject.

Perversion is approached from such contrasting standpoints that its psychopathological significance is easily lost sight of. Perhaps the inconsistency of the various approaches stems from the fact that the symptom of "perversion" has so many different meanings that it calls for a variety of observational perspectives. However, this multi-sidedness cannot justify the tendency to generalize from or base theories on what may be regarded purely as clinical or therapeutic options.

Hence, it seemed to me important to shift the focus from the clinical level to that of theory in order to identify the points of agreement and disagreement on the sadomasochistic perversion and the theoretical foundations of the various positions. I was faced, therefore, with the problem of where to place the subject within the present-day spectrum of psychoanalysis—no easy matter in this age of "many psychoanalyses" existing side by side.

The attempt to outline the broad theoretical currents originating from a small number of founding fathers (or mothers) without oversimplification proved to be quite complicated. Nor did it seem useful, for the purposes of my specific subject, to reconstruct the complex geographical, cultural or historical reasons for the broad panoply of psychoanalytic theories with which we are confronted today.

My first finding was that theory reflects unchanged, but on a more abstract level, the divergences already encountered in clinical work. The theoretical standpoints underlying the various clinical approaches appear so remote from each other that radically differing developmental and prognostic meanings seem to have been assigned to perversion. Each psychoanalytic conception of perversion seems to cover only a part of its changing and multiform nature, so that, paradoxically, it may be useful and even desirable to adopt a multi-centred approach.

As I went on, another reason for the complexity and difficulty of investigating the nature of perversion emerged. Even though psychoanalysis has from the beginning attributed enormous importance to sexuality, to the extent of basing an entire theory of human development on it, psychoanalysts, like researchers in other disciplines, find themselves unable to penetrate in depth its intimate essence.

Human sexuality is generally held to be determined by not only biological but also psychological factors, and it is acknowledged that we still know very little about the role of the latter in the processes of an individual's love life and the development of his or her sexual imagination. It is hard to identify what is natural and what is learned in human sexual behaviour, just as it is not easy to comprehend the processes leading to sexual differentiation.

For example, if we were closer to comprehending the underlying causes of the diversity of the psychic and imaginative components of normal male and female sexuality, perhaps we should also come a little nearer to the understanding of perversion, whose mystery reflects the equally unfathomable enigma of desire and the choice of sexual object.

If we are to make significant progress in studying the subject of perversion, we must investigate the nature of sexuality in greater depth and arrive at a more exhaustive idea of the dynamics and context of orgasmic pleasure.

To gain a better understanding of the central importance of sexual pleasure and the power it exerts over the psychic life of the individual, I felt it essential to start from the experience of sexuality in itself, and initially to adopt a phenomenological and experiential approach, refraining as far as possible from any psychodynamic type of theorization. For it seems to me that such theorization can easily lead to a misunderstanding of the significance of human sexuality, which, whether included to excess in theories (in the form of psychosexuality) or, conversely, regarded as an epiphenomenon of the affective bond between persons (in theories of object relations or relational theories), has come to assume differing and irreconcilable psychoanalytic statuses.

Whereas extension of the concept of the sexual drive leads to denial of the differences between normal and pathological behaviour, excessive emphasis on the psychological dimension tends to obscure the specificity and autonomy of the sexual sphere.

I contend that the perverse experience, while retaining some continuity with shared sexuality, cannot be equated with or integrated in it. I therefore take issue with psychoanalytic theories that see perverse components as belonging to normal sexuality or consider perversion as including aspects potentially compatible with the affective and relational world.

As to the social field, in the last few decades perversion has emerged from the closet and become a group phenomenon in search of a seal of approval. Past phobic visions of sex, which relegated perverse sexuality to anonymity and secrecy, are no more, and seem to have now been superseded by a subtly ambiguous position that portrays a dose of "winking" transgression as the exercise of freedom. The aim of this communal organization is to remove perversion from the realm of solitary practice and, by strengthening the sexual identity of its protagonists, to increase their number. I do not regard perverse aspects in search of social confirmation as one of the variants of ordinary sexuality today. Perversion, in my view, remains the same, even if the form of social aggregation and the visibility of a long-submerged and misunderstood phenomenon have changed.

My own position avoids, on the one hand, the simple attribution of deviance to perversion and, on the other, the simplifying acceptance of "a measure of abnormality".[1]

If new views are to be elaborated we must adopt an eccentric position with regard to established psychoanalytic theories and temporarily forget what has already been said. Moreover, my approach aims to purge the concept of perversion of a set of semantic accretions that have broadened its field disproportionately and sometimes denatured its meaning.

Metaphorically speaking, my aim is the isolation, within a complex organism, of a cell that I call the "sadomasochistic monad", in which I place the mental experience of destructive pleasure.

The sadomasochistic perversion thus emerges as a staging post on the way to a complex mental universe in which a certain type of pleasure is established as a single compulsive act. My description therefore emphasizes the dangerous and extreme aspect—the aspect that coincides with the sexualization of destructive pleasure. However, I do not neglect the fact that perverse behaviour or the acting out of fantasies often constitutes a transitional act symptomatic of other experiences, in which pleasure may be connected with the traumatic unpleasure of past negative experiences.

Another equally important issue is whether, among the numerous symptomatic and non-symptomatic expressions of sadomasochism, sexual perversion pure and simple can be distinguished. After all, analysts in their clinical practice encounter many manifestations of perverse fantasy in a variety of psychopathological contexts, but are seldom confronted with an actual, structured, sexual perversion.

The psychoanalytic study of the sadomasochistic perversion is hampered by the dearth of information based on clinical experience, since it is quite rare for a perverse individual to request psycho-analytic treatment.

The psychoanalyst is more likely to encounter perverse fantasies, especially of a masochistic type and sometimes confined to the moment of sexual intercourse, in persons (mainly women) who have to come to terms with their frigidity and whose lack of sexual pleasure is connected with traumatic infantile experiences. Although it is said that there is no such thing as sadism without masochistic aspects, I think it appropriate to isolate and distinguish a purely masochistic position, which may result from repeated traumatic experiences. Whereas in sadomasochism the positions may be constantly reversed, in these cases the only possible configuration is the erotization of submission, in which the subject never has any desire to assume the dominant position.

It is not unusual for a borderline patient, tormented by anxiety at the possibility of losing control over his mind in relation to the perverse experience that both attracts and terrifies him, to ask for psychoanalytic help. Here, too, however, the clinical picture is one in which the symptom of perversion is just one of the problems arising in a complex structure of balances and defences against anxiety.

One reason for the scarcity of relevant psychoanalytic case histories is that the customary grounds for confidentiality here become absolute, as a rule making it impossible to use the clinical material concerned where, as is often the case, it relates to highly secret and personal situations. The student of sadomasochism must therefore not only listen to his own patients but also be capable of utilizing documentary sources, such as autobiographical accounts, pornographic literature and certain types of films, which will help him to come into contact with those who are attracted by the link between the pleasure of domination and the pain of submission and have borne witness to it. My exposition thus also draws freely on literary testimony and autobiographical experiences.

The reading of such texts, not only corroborates and enriches the material we may hear and understand from patients during psychoanalytic sessions, but also bears out the fact that the perverse experience, notwithstanding the diversity of the characters involved and the complexity of each individual's imagination, takes the form of a "cell" possessing certain constant basic characteristics. This aspect not only characterizes perversion but also—despite the disguises it dons and the infinite variations accompanying it—gives it a repetitive, monotonous quality, invisible only to the pervert owing to the excitation that fuels it.

In this investigation, I emphasize the mysterious nature of the sadomasochistic perversion and the congruence of the psychoanalytic theories that attempt to explain it. Like other fields of knowledge, in which new scientific paradigms succeed each other or coexist in time, the present-day psychoanalytic landscape includes a number of mutually complementary models or parameters for the interpretation of clinical reality. I have done my best to examine exhaustively each of the successive psychoanalytic hypotheses on the subject, including those now current, as well as the premises underlying the ideas of the different authors who, despite their differing theoretical allegiances, agree on certain fundamental points.

In this connection, it should be recalled that the dynamic of perversion was used by Freud very creatively in his account of the early development of the infantile libido and in his hypothesis that there is a "background" of perversion in each of us; hence there remains the Freudian theory of the perversions according to which perversion is closely bound up with psychosexual development (cf. *Three Essays on the Theory of Sexuality*, 1905d; "A child is being beaten", 1919e; The economic problem of masochism, 1924c).

The Kleinian approach represents a departure from this theory. For its protagonists, the death drive underlies psychopathological structures, and perversion is one of the areas in which these structures operate and reinforce each other through sexualization, omnipotence and pleasure in the destructive domination of the other.

Other authors, who espouse relational theories, regard perversion—seen predominantly as an erotized form of relationship as a defence against catastrophic anxieties—as an existential strategy that may later develop into forms of integration of the personality.

In this book I shall review the principal theoretical contributions (those of Chasseguet-Smirgel (1984), Khan (1979) and Meltzer (1973) to mention only a few of the best known authors), because I believe that, notwithstanding the progress achieved in the psychoanalytic investigation of perversion, many areas of this phenomenon remain elusive and are not accounted for by our present-day conceptualization. Indeed, excessive dependence on theoretical models seems to preclude actual observation of the perverse experience, and may in some cases even lead to distortion of the sense of the observable data.

Although psychoanalysis is the discipline that allows the deepest understanding of the perverse experience, systematic observation of that experience is, as stated, rare in clinical practice. It is therefore not legitimate to generalize from individual psychoanalytic treatments, which should involve prolonged periods of well-structured therapy in addition to finely constructed theoretical models. The dynamic approach reveals the sexual perversions as coexisting with other underlying psychopathological structures, and shows how other pathologies can use mechanisms of the perverse type.

I have attempted to restrict the field of perversion to the sexual sphere, although I am aware that the symptom "perversion" is also manifested in other psychopathological experiences, such as, for example, sexualized states in psychosis, acting out in borderline pathologies, sexualized defences in depression, or disturbances of sexual life resulting from infantile traumas.

Finally, I have devoted particular attention to the areas of contiguity between perversion and other mental conditions, such as psychosis or criminality, and have attempted to identify a link between borderline structures and compulsive perversion.

Notes

1. An allusion to the title of a book on perversion by Joyce McDougall (1980).

CHAPTER TWO

A precursor

The study of deviant sexuality began at the end of the nineteenth century with the publication of the first edition of Krafft-Ebing's voluminous treatise *Psychopathia Sexualis* (1886–1902), in which the sexual aberrations were for the first time deemed an object worthy of psychiatric study. The book contains an abundance of case histories covering the entire range of sexual deviations, including the most extreme.

It has been pointed out (Grossman, 1986) that the definition and scientific study of the sadomasochistic perversion predated the birth of psychoanalysis by a decade and decisively influenced the development of that discipline.[1]

For Krafft-Ebing, whose oeuvre resembles a huge fresco many times revised and extended, the fundamental form of all deviations was reflected in sadism and masochism, which represented the active and passive aspects respectively of the drive of subjugation. The choice of perversion was always latent, even where its onset could be documented in specific episodes in infancy. Krafft-Ebing believed that an event in infancy, such as the young Rousseau's excitement when he was beaten (which Freud also mentions), was only a secondary factor in the aetiology of masochism—the occasion for its emergence rather than its cause.

Many passages in Freud's *Three Essays on the Theory of Sexuality* (1905d) paraphrase some of Krafft-Ebing's generalizations—for example, those on the continuity between the normal and the pathological, the ubiquity of the influence of sexuality on human behaviour and thought, and the coexistence of primitive and adult levels of sexuality.

Endowed with an abundant psychological intuition that enabled him to penetrate deeper than his contemporaries (Kerr, 1993, p. 92f.), Krafft-Ebing drew attention to the importance of early infantile sexual experiences in the development of perverse sexuality, and had the insight that the deviant masturbatory fantasies of infancy underlay the development of perversion in adulthood: "by a transference through associations of ideas", the sexual attraction of part of the body could be displaced on to a fetish. Krafft-Ebing knew that certain "fancies" originated in early infancy and could not be satisfied in actuality because "the whole thing chiefly belongs to the realm of the imagination". He also held that a masochistic fantasy could be "latent" and remain the "unconscious motive" hidden behind the fetish. He was certainly aware of infantile masturbation, of the "erogenous" zones, including the anus, of the sexual significance of sucking at the nipple, and of the role of shame and disgust in sexual education.

In his view, those destined for perversion were sexually hyperexcitable and predisposed to "sexual ecstasy".

Long before Freud, Krafft-Ebing believed in the intimate connection between polarities such as sadism/masochism and male/female, as well as in the bisexual disposition of human beings. The male, he thought, being more active and aggressive, developed in the sadistic direction, whereas the female reproduced the masochistic element. Male masochism represented a form of sexual inversion in which, in view of the potential for bisexuality, a feminine attitude was transferred to a man.

For all the keenness of some of his intuitions, Krafft-Ebing did not succeed in formulating an appropriate theory of perversion; unlike Freud, he lacked a conceptual apparatus that could draw a line of demarcation between mental health and illness and distinguish between constitutional factors and early environmental experiences. This shortcoming prevented him from casting off the organicist heritage of the medicine of his time, and in particular the theory of hereditary degeneration and of the importance of organic factors (such as epilepsy).

In his case histories the development of a perverse tendency is sometimes attributed to events in infancy and linked to the relationship with a family member, whereas on other occasions the infantile experience is seen as a first manifestation of the hereditary degeneration that would unfold fully in adulthood.

Although it paved the way for the Freudian revolution, Krafft-Ebing's scientific work was forgotten by those who followed in the footsteps of the founder of psychoanalysis, the discipline in which it was further developed. The oblivion that has befallen his oeuvre has strengthened the impression that the entire scientific revolution that unfolded and crystallized around the interpretation of sexuality and its aberrations arose in the mind of Freud, whereas Freud actually owed some of the truths underlying important psychoanalytic intuitions to Krafft-Ebing and others.

Note

1. Krafft-Ebing himself sent a copy of his treatise to Freud whenever a new edition came out, and certain passages were duly underlined. The two men respected each other (Sulloway, 1979). In a footnote on the first page of the *Three Essays on the Theory of Sexuality* (1905d), Freud acknowledged that much of his knowledge of this field was derived from the work of Krafft-Ebing, Moll, Möbius, Ellis, Schrenck-Notzing, Löwenfeld, Eulenburg, Bloch and Hirschfeld.

CHAPTER THREE

Problems of terminology and definition

I n the field of deviation, any behaviour falling outside the social norm was traditionally deemed pathological. This was the case with sexual perversion. The concept of perversion is ambiguous and open to criticism on many accounts—in particular, because in the course of time its definition has increasingly been characterized by moral or normative considerations.

The term perversion, which denotes a deviation from the norm, tells us nothing about the origin, context or nature of the process concerned. The descriptive criterion, which refers to the sum of the usual behaviour leading to procreation, does not facilitate the understanding of the problem. If the norm of sexual behaviour consisted only in sexual relations ending with coitus and the introduction of the penis into the vagina, many sexual experiences —for example, simple masturbation—would be perverse in character. A century ago, Krafft-Ebing pointed out that the key to the diagnosis of perversion was not so much the act itself as the entire personality of the individual concerned and the specific motivation of the perverse act.

A more appropriate method, commonly used in the psychoanalytic study of perversion, is to compare it with the love relationship that accompanies sexual exchanges between partners. This type of sexuality characterizes those persons, deemed to be mature or well integrated, who seek sexual pleasure within a relationship of love and affection. Sexuality in these cases is not impulsive, and satisfaction can be postponed until the conditions for an intimate relationship are created: the pleasure stems from the enjoyment offered to the partner and from the pleasure sought by the subject himself.

In other words, relational love consists in a harmonious and balanced meeting of the search for personal gratification with an altruistic attention to and respect for the pleasure of the other. In other situations, however, the sexual impulse demands immediate satisfaction, thus revealing a disjunction between sexuality and love. This disjunctive process is quite common in ordinary sexuality, where a certain oscillation between the two positions—affectionate love and purely sexual love—is observed; this oscillation is a universal physiological characteristic, which confirms that sexuality and orgasm are variable components independent of love.

Leaving the field of affectionate, passionate love and moving on to that of love considered as pure sexual satisfaction and gratification, we observe sexuality dominated by aggressive components, i.e. the sadistic sexual universe. The penis becomes a conquering, penetrating weapon; possession of the sexual object, which is controlled and subjugated, becomes pure narcissistic gratification sustained by contempt. Deviant sexuality belongs to the world of excitation and pornography and has its roots in aggressive fantasy. Love for the other ceases to exist, and gives way to the excitation of triumph and power. Even if aggressive sexuality is not completely identical with perversion, aggressive sexual pleasure is the breeding ground of sadomasochism.

In psychoanalytic terms, every perversion involves a process of degradation of the love object, whereby the person is transformed into a thing. In fetishism, for example, the vehicle of sexual imagination is the concrete object, which replaces a human object.

This process only takes place in sadomasochism in an extreme and consistent form and, in continuity with the other perversions, is based on a form of imagination from which the symbolic and emotional are banished and which, to a greater extent than other perversions, presents an uncompromising configuration of the pleasure of possession and domination. The sadomasochist must destroy the object's humanity and enslave the object in order to derive pleasure from it. The dehumanization is a consequence of the power principle: to be usable, the object must become a thing.

The uncertainty of definition outlined above also affects the terminology, which appears quite lacking in expressiveness when compared with the nature of perversion. Let me emphasize again that the term "perversion" is not only inappropriate but also derogatory and laden with moral prejudices. In the developing debate of the last few years, the term "perverse", already banished from psychiatric nosography, has also tended to disappear from psychoanalytic language.

The recent trend is evidenced by the attitudes and debates within the American Psychiatric Association, which have crystallized in the formulation of the successive editions of its *Diagnostic and Statistical Manual of Mental Disorders* (*DSM*). Whereas the first two editions still referred to pathological sexuality and sexual deviations, in the third the two categories, this time described as identity disturbances and paraphilias, are placed under the heading of psychosexual disturbances. The term "paraphilia" is retained in *DSM-IV* (1994), which enumerates "Sexual dysfunction", "Paraphilia" and "Gender identity disorder".

The psychiatric category of perversion may be said to have undergone many changes, but these, however, are perhaps less radical than those concerning the concept of homosexuality, which has been expunged once and for all from the psychiatric vocabulary of the *DSM, even in the form of "ego-dystonic homosexuality"*.

The paraphilias include all the traditional perversions, such as fetishism, transvestism, exhibitionism, voyeurism, paedophilia, sadomasochism, and so on.

The term "paraphilia" is neutral and, unlike "perversion", lacks moral connotations, so that it cannot be suspected of having the aim of labelling those who are "different" as wicked or contemptible. Even so, I prefer not to use it because on the one hand it is to my mind too anodyne and generic, while on the other it suggests a link with love-related components. The Greek etymon "-philia" seems to me to be totally inappropriate when applied to sadomasochism.

In spite of the element of moral prejudice inherent in the term, I therefore prefer to speak of *perversion*. I feel very close to Stoller (1985), who sees an action as perverse when the erotic excitation depends on the individual's sense of sinning. The concept of sin, which is based on the individual's consciousness and emotional perception, is not scientific, just as it is not scientific to assert that people do not believe in sin.

The notion of sin is central to perversion because it stresses the subjective perception of the transgressive action out of which the pleasure arises. The wish to transgress the moral order, to humiliate, to subvert or to be cruel, which is felt to be "natural" in the individual pervert, constitutes the only possible form of sexual imagination.

In the extensive field of "sexual aberrations", Stoller distinguishes the "variants", which are not guided by conscious intentions, from the "perversions" proper, which result from a conscious hostile motivation or from the wish to expose oneself to risk (as, for example, in exhibitionism). These subjective components are the prerequisites of sexual orgasm. Sadomasochistic individuals do not at all deny their "perversity", since they are fully aware that their excitation arises out of the pleasure of injustice and exploitation, whether acted out or undergone.

The term "sadism" was proposed by Krafft-Ebing himself to denote the union between sexual pleasure and cruelty, the latter ranging from moral humiliation to physical destruction of the other. The emblematic reference was the life and literary oeuvre of the Marquis de Sade.

At about the same time, Schrenk-Notzing (1895) had suggested the term "algolagnia" (active or passive), from the Greek *algos* (pain) and *lagneia* (lust); this word united the two poles of the perversion, with the stress laid on pain. Owing to the extension and variety of the fantasies and behaviours included in the perversion, however, the emphasis on pain appeared to be a limiting element, so that the term sadomasochism, derived from the names of the two famous authors notorious for their sexual practices, ultimately prevailed. The definition of masochism was not confined to physical pain but also included mental or moral distress such as degradation and humiliation.

The clear definition of masochism given by Krafft-Ebing (1902) is still valid today:

By masochism I understand a peculiar perversion of the psychical vita sexualis in which the individual affected, in sexual feeling and thought, is controlled by the idea of being completely and unconditionally subject to the will of a person of the opposite sex; of being treated by this person as by a master, humiliated and abused. This idea is coloured by lustful feeling; the masochist lives in fancies, in which he creates situations of this kind and often attempts to realize them. [Krafft-Ebing, 1902; quoted in Arndt, 1991, p. 352]

The observation that the sadist is not interested either in cruelty or in pain outside the sexual sphere is due to Havelock Ellis (1913). Whereas cruelty is always present in sadism, not all forms of cruelty can be identified with sadism. Krafft-Ebing stresses the preponderant role of submission and humiliation, not of pain. Even in the sexual act, the pervert wishes not to inflict pain or suffering, but rather to feel that the victim wishes to suffer, in order to attain orgasm. For the sadist, it is important to think that pain and submission produce pleasure and that the partner enjoys what is done to him.

For sadism is the expression of the sexual excitement of triumph and power and not of suffering inflicted on the other. A generalization to the effect that every form of submissive behaviour is a manifestation of masochism, sometimes to be found in psychoanalytic-type publications, confuses rather than clarifies the field of perverse sexual behaviour.

Psychoanalytic literature commonly refers more to physical and mental pain and to cruelty rather than to humiliation and submission (see Brenner, 1959; Loewenstein, 1957), so that Krafft-Ebing's definition is disregarded (Arndt, 1991); the sexual character of masochism frequently goes by the board, the term itself being used generically for all situations in which punishment or defeat is sought. Finally, besides the indiscriminate use of the individual perversion and of individual polarities (masochism or sadism), we also observe a broadening of the concept of perversion itself.

However, it was Freud himself who, step by step, extended the metapsychological significance of masochism. Whereas in 1905 (Three Essays on the Theory of Sexuality) he placed sadomasochism in the context of infantile sexuality in the specific sense of a sexual aberration, in 1919 ("A child is being beaten") he focused on the exploration of the underlying Oedipal fantasy and the position of submission to the father. This paper shows that masochists develop a particular susceptibility in regard to father figures and that, in spite of themselves, they create situations that bring about concrete sadomasochistic bonds.

In 1924 ("The economic problem of masochism"), Freud extended the analysis of masochism to include the moral field and the feminine character. This widening of the theoretical and metapsychological horizon created a conceptual unity covering a variety of clinical forms, such as sexual, moral and feminine masochism.

The changing perspective on the concept of masochism exemplifies the way in which a psychoanalytic idea comes into being, is transformed and may then dissolve (Grossman, 1986).

An extension that is in my view unwarranted is made by Kaplan (1991), who includes cases of anorexia, bulimia and other behaviours such as self-mutilation and kleptomania under "perversion".

The fact that one and the same term describes both a sexual behaviour and a desexualized dynamic greatly dilutes the concept of sadomasochism: the term is used in a general and descriptive sense, that of ordinary language, to denote any state of excessive submission and suffering, without regard to the quality of the suffering or the specific dynamic of perversion.

Masochism sometimes generically denotes passivity (Grossman, 1986). The term sadism and masochism are indeed applied in psychoanalysis both to the sexual perversion and to non-sexual character pathologies, as well as to a wide range of behaviours, thoughts and attitudes. Depending on the author concerned, the term may refer to a variety of concepts, such as a very severe superego, aggressive conflicts, anal–sadistic fixations, symbiotic dependence, or feminine traits (Maleson, 1984), thus wrongly suggesting the existence of similarities between fundamentally heterogeneous entities.

Other authors extend the term "perverse" to the description of certain personality traits or types of relationships, thus imbuing it with non-sexual implications and bringing it increasingly close to the concept of distortion, overturning or perverting what is real, true or right.

Human relations enter the field of sadomasochism when contempt and devaluation accompany the pleasure of inflicting suffering and of suffering as a victim: in these cases, continuous tormenting of the other and of the subject himself is paradoxically preferred to separation. In all these cases it would in my view be better to speak of "perversity", and to reserve the term "perversion" for sexual behaviour.

A wider perspective on perversion is afforded by the contribution of certain analysts on the alteration of the perception of psychic reality and the consequences of the disavowal entailed by perversion.

Chasseguet-Smirgel (1985), for example, describes how reality is perverted through denial of the differences between the sexes and generations: in perversion, psychic reality is fragmented and mixed, like faeces, in which all differences, including the difference between good and bad, are abolished. Typical of perversion is the creation of an ideal world involving not only the denial of sexual and generational differences but also the conviction of the absence of separation, time and death.

The British post-Kleinian authors (Meltzer, 1973; Rosenfeld, 1988), for their part, concentrate on perverse relations between parts of the personality in pathological organizations. In these organizations, destructive narcissistic nuclei (represented in dreams by delinquent gangs) take control of and overpower the healthy parts, which are made to acquiesce in their submission (Steiner, 1982).

The psychic state in these circumstances ultimately takes the form of a struggle between parts of the personality, similar to that observable in sadomasochistic sexuality. These destructive parts often afford a retreat or refuge replete with narcissistic qualities, which provides relief from anxiety and pain (Steiner, 1993), but which more frequently (Rosenfeld, 1971) constitutes a perverse structure that captures the other parts of the self.

CHAPTER FOUR

Sadomasochism and depression

A ccording to Abraham's contributions on depression (1911, 1916, 1924), the suffering of melancholia arises out of the patient's perception of a self capable of hating rather than loving. That is why melancholia, unlike mourning, includes conscious hate for the subject's own self.

In "Mourning and melancholia" (1916–1917g [1915]), Freud takes up this essential aspect of unconscious hate and places it in the perspective of a sadomasochistic relationship that is both internal and external.

Unlike a bereaved person, the melancholic feels not only that his world has become meaningless but also that his ego has been emptied out. In confirmation of his own unworthiness, he attributes to himself not merely guilt but all the negative qualities of the world, too. Freud points out that, in melancholia, it is not just the relationship with the lost love object that is altered, as in mourning, but in addition the relationship with the subject's own ego. Whereas in mourning the loss concerns the object, in melancholia it is the ego itself that is affected.

To explain the case in which hate is directed not only towards the world but also against the subject's own ego, Freud hypothesizes that the patient has had a traumatic early relationship with the love object. After this trauma, the melancholic distances himself from his own object, internalizing it as a source of perpetual suffering and conflict, and tends to establish relationships of dependence moulded by this traumatic event. The primal feeling of not being loved gives rise to a constant reproach to the love object, which is accused of insufficiency and unworthiness. This drama is repeated in every relationship.

The love object, being unable to make up for the primal offence, thus always remains open to criticism and attack. The constant accusations make it impossible to assess the real shortcomings so that they can be distinguished from presumed ones.

In this way, there comes into being an object relationship with a sadomasochistic character, in which the sadistic side takes the form of repeated accusations of imperfection directed at the object, and the masochistic side that of the adoption of the victim's position of unhappiness: the melancholic tortures the object, by which he in turn feels tortured.

In Freud's view, the accusations directed at the love object are really those directed by the ego at itself, because it is totally identified with the object. Hence the victimization and torture inflicted by the melancholic on himself. The powerful adhesive identification with the love object enables us to understand the suicidal dynamics of the melancholic, whose destructiveness, even when turned against himself, is directed vengefully at the love object in a sadomasochistic vicious circle.

In this context it is also easy to understand why actual mourning may give rise to a melancholic state. The reparative processes intended to make good the loss by the working through of the hate for the painful reality are very difficult for the melancholic, whose primal relationship with the love object is imbued with resentment and feelings of revenge.

The relationship between the conscience (superego) and the ego, too, assumes a sadomasochistic character in melancholia. Every loss constitutes an offence that unleashes the sadistic attack on the object and is consequently reintrojected into the ego, which in turn becomes the masochistic object of the superego.

The melancholic's superego sadistically inflicts punishments on the ego, which willingly receives them. Freud (in the wake of

Abraham) notes how the behaviour of the melancholic, who punishes himself for his deficiencies and confesses his unworthiness, is far from consistent, in that it is devoid of humility both in his life and in his relationship with the analyst. Melancholics are often openly arrogant and destructive, thus amply demonstrating that the self-criticism with which they torment themselves is not so much an assumption of responsibility as a secret and exciting pleasure.

My reason for giving this summary of the problem complex of melancholia and its sadomasochistic element is to draw attention to what I believe to be the fundamental aspect of the level on which the sadomasochistic experience belongs when manifested in nonsexual relations or the psychic world. The sadomasochistic relationship is in my view the prototype of many relationships that turn out to be clinging and hard to dissolve. Hate, after all, may unite to a greater extent than love.

It is, in my view, very important to describe the (object-related) interpersonal dynamics that characterize sadomasochistic relationships and distinguish them from the specific elements of sexual perversion proper.

An extensive body of psychoanalytic literature following on from Freud and Abraham has attempted to show that sexual perversions are the outcome of conflicts between different psychical agencies (the ego and superego in particular). I myself take a different view—namely, that the masochistic perversion must, in fact, in order to pave the way for sexual pleasure, obliterate any conflictual problems, whether conscious or unconscious. Pure sexual perversion does not stem from conflicts, but is actually characterized by agreement and syntony between the various parts of the self.

It is one thing to speak of sadomasochistic interpersonal dynamics, but another to draw analogies with sexual perversion. The assertion that the pervert tends to entertain personal relationships in line with his sexual disturbance does not correspond to reality. On the contrary, someone—for example, the melancholic—who constantly creates sadomasochistic relationships keeps himself well away from the world of sexual perversion.

CHAPTER FIVE

Feminine masochism, or the case of the Wolf Man

T o assist further in resolving the confusion between perversion and neurotic behaviour, let us now examine the use and meaning of the sadomasochistic position in the clinical treatment of the neuroses as inspired by the theory of psychosexual development.

In my view, Freud gives a clearer and more scientifically consistent description of the sadomasochistic relationship when he considers the object relationship of the melancholic or moral masochism ("The economic problem of masochism", 1924c). Conversely, where he describes personality aspects bordering on constitutional characteristics (male/female or active/passive), as in the case of feminine masochism or the homosexual position, his hypotheses appear far shakier and less useful.

As stated earlier, Freud's theory of feminine masochism is based on a scientific prejudice typical of his time—so much so that it was even shared by Krafft-Ebing. Freud uses this concept in an attempt to explain one of the components of sexual masochism and certain aspects of homosexuality: the homosexual is unconsciously identified with a woman who passively submits.

To illustrate these dynamics appropriately, I have chosen to discuss the Wolf Man (Freud, 1918b [1914]), one of Freud's most comprehensive case histories.

It is common knowledge that this patient's first analysis was incomplete. The treatment, which had seemingly restored him to a state of well being, did not resolve certain elements of his pathology, including severe psychosomatic symptoms and a devastating existential anxiety. The patient had more analysis with Freud himself in 1920 and was then entrusted to his pupil Ruth Mack Brunswick, who wrote a further clinical account.

Although Freud did not regard the Wolf Man as a serious case, both his history and Mack Brunswick's report of his subsequent treatment suggest that he was in all probability a borderline and not merely neurotic.

I shall consider here the conclusion of the first part of the therapy, as recorded by Freud in 1914.

Owing to the persistence in the analysis of an attitude of docile indifference and passivity (the patient listened attentively to what was said to him but did not show any progress), Freud was compelled to take a radical decision—namely, to inform the patient that he intended to terminate the analysis by a set date. Under the pressure of this deadline, the patient's resistance disappeared, as did his symptoms, and his inhibitions were resolved. Meanwhile the patient produced some very interesting material, as a result of which Freud felt that he had got to the root of the treatment. The favourable outcome of the therapy confirmed to him the validity of the sexual basis of neurotic symptoms and the traumatic and exciting significance of the primal scene, contained in the famous dream of the wolves.

I am recapitulating the case of the Wolf Man because it centres on the reconstruction of the infantile neurosis and therefore seems particularly suitable for demonstrating Freud's conception of the role of sadomasochism in psychosexual development.

In his reconstruction of the patient's history, Freud thought that, as a child, the Wolf Man had felt compelled to give up masturbation on account of castration anxiety. For this reason, his psychosexuality crystallized in the form of an anal–sadistic organization. He became irritable and petulant, and enjoyed tormenting animals and people. He began to commit acts of cruelty against small animals, catching flies and pulling their wings off. In his fantasy, he imagined himself beating horses. There were also unequivocally sadistic fantasies, including one of children being punished and beaten, particularly on the penis. Another frequent fantasy was of an heir to the throne who was locked up in a cell and beaten. The heir to the throne was certainly himself: the sadism was thus turned against the patient himself and transformed into masochism. Freud writes (1918b [1914], p. 26): "No doubt was left in the analysis that these passive trends had made their appearance at the same time as the active-sadistic ones, or very soon after them", and adds in a footnote: "By passive trends I mean trends that have a passive sexual aim; but in saying this I have in mind a transformation not of the instinct but only of its aim" (ibid., n. 2).

The detail of the punishment inflicted directly on the genital organ suggested to Freud that the patient also felt guilty about his masturbation. The patient's masochistic trends drove him to approach the Oedipal conflict and the relationship with his father in the form of erotized submission. Freud continues:

We have heard already that his father had been his admired model [...]. This object of identification of his active current became the sexual object of a passive current in his present anal–sadistic phase. [...] His father was now his object once more [...]; while the transformation of his active attitude into a passive one was the consequence and the record of the seduction which had occurred meanwhile. [ibid., p. 27]

During this period, the child's screaming fits or "naughtiness" were put in the service of masochistic intentions: he exhibited his naughtiness so as to force his father to punish or beat him, so as ultimately to obtain the desired masochistic satisfaction.

The fits thus constituted attempts at seduction: "In accordance, moreover, with the motives which underlie masochism, this beating would also have satisfied his sense of guilt. [...] He hopes for a beating as a simultaneous means of setting his sense of guilt at rest and of satisfying his masochistic sexual trend" (ibid., p. 28).

Again, of the wishes that gave rise to the famous dream of the wolves, the most powerful must have been that for sexual satisfaction from the father: "The strength of this wish made it possible to revive a long-forgotten trace in his memory of a scene which was able to show him what sexual satisfaction from his father was like" (ibid., p. 35).

As we know, Freud traced this dream back to an occasion when the patient was 18 months old, linking it to a scene of parental intercourse which took place in somewhat unusual circumstances that were especially favourable for the child's observation:

> His anxiety [in the dream] was a repudiation of the wish for sexual satisfaction from his father [...]. [...] the fear of "being eaten by the wolf", was only the (as we shall hear, regressive) transposition of the wish to be copulated with by his father, that is, to be given sexual satisfaction in the same way as his mother. His last sexual aim, the passive attitude towards his father, succumbed to repression, and fear of his father appeared in its place in the shape of the wolf phobia. [...] [The sexual aim] was then transformed, by regression to the earlier stage of the sadistic–anal organization, into the masochistic aim of being beaten or punished. It was a matter of indifference to him whether he reached this aim with a man or with a woman. [...] The activation of the primal scene in the dream now brought him back to the genital organization. He discovered the vagina and the biological significance of masculine and feminine. He understood now that active was the same as masculine, while passive was the same as feminine. His passive sexual aim should now have been transformed into a feminine one, and have expressed itself as "being copulated with by his father" instead of "being beaten by him on the genitals or on the bottom". This feminine aim, however, underwent repression and was obliged to let itself be replaced by fear of the wolf. [*ibid.*, p. 46]

Freud later sets out even more clearly the problem of the relationship between the patient's masochistic position and his unconscious homosexuality:

> The operation of the dream, which brought him under the influence of the primal scene, could have led him [...] to transform his masochism towards his father into a feminine attitude towards him—into homosexuality. [...] His relation to his father might have been expected to proceed from the sexual aim of being beaten by him to the next aim, namely, that of being copulated with by him like a woman. [*ibid.*, p. 64]

Homosexuality would therefore have represented a more advanced phase of psychosexual development than the masochistic position, but the patient could not attain it owing to his anxiety about being devoured (castrated) by the wolf (father).

The above passages from the case history of the Wolf Man contain both a part of the theory of psychosexual development and Freud's outline of the genesis of perversion.

On the one hand, sadism and masochism are regarded as a phase of psychosexual development: in the anal–sadistic phase, the drive can only have a given form of expression and a given object-related aim. This anal–sadistic organization may constitute a nucleus of pathogenic fantasies, which ultimately come to be fixed and may assume the form of an actual perversion in adult life.

The Wolf Man, as he approaches the genital position but fails to reach it, certainly develops a pathology but not a sexual perversion.

Sadomasochism is portrayed as one of the expressions and aims of the libidinal forces preceding the Oedipus complex.

For Freud, then, the entities of "sadism" and "masochism" flow together into the larger crucible of psychosexuality, of the formation of sexual identity in its final forms (masculine/feminine, active/passive), variants (homosexuality) and pathology (the sadomasochistic perversion).

To interpret some of the patient's many psychosomatic symptoms, such as his intestinal disorders, Freud resorted to a similar model based on the equivalence of passivity and femininity on the one hand and of activity and masculinity on the other. Using a memory of the patient's in which the mother complained of uterine haemorrhages and pains, Freud maintained that the child had unconsciously identified with her:

> Under the influence of the primal scene he came to the conclusion that his mother had been made ill by what his father had done to her; and his dread of having blood in his stool, of being as ill as his mother, was his repudiation of being identified with her in this sexual scene [...]. But the dread was also a proof that in his later elaboration of the primal scene he had put himself in his mother's place and had envied her this relation with his father. [*ibid.*, p. 78]

CHAPTER SIX

Ascetic masochism

T he phenomenon of ascetic masochism is worthy of separate consideration.

M. R. Bell's book *Holy Anorexia* (1985) includes an account of the life of the late-thirteenth-century Dominican nun Benvenuta Boianni, whose biography has come down to us through the notes taken by her confessor. Benvenuta embarked on her ascetic career in the conviction that she could achieve union with God only by following the path of suffering.

The masochistic determination by which Benvenuta characterized her life first became evident in adolescence: from the age of 12, she began to practise systematic self-flagellation and to bind her body tightly with a rope that cut into her flesh and injured it. Every so often, St Dominic would appear to her and interrupt her torments; advising her to speak to her confessor, he offered her a voice that removed her temporarily from the instruments of torture. Divine and demoniac presences alternated in her, with the demon as a being impelling her towards sexual desire and pleasure. Benvenuta refused food for long periods, and in one of these prolonged fasts she fell seriously ill and nearly died.

With the inextricable combination of her wish for perfection, pleasure in suffering, and sense of guilt and persecution, in line with the religious expectations and cultural climate of the time, Benvenuta became an extraordinary being—a saint.

However, the ascetic journey towards the infinite and divine through the suffering of physical pain seemed to Benvenuta on her deathbed to be so catastrophically reprehensible that her guilt precluded any possibility of salvation.

It was thus only as she lay dying that she became aware of the destructive spirit that had ruled her life: she was afraid that, because of all the self-inflicted mortifications whereby she had accelerated her death, she would be condemned to suffer perpetual torment instead of enjoying eternal life.

In a fascinating little book, *The Art of Starvation*, McLeod (1981) gives an account of her experience as an anorexic. Writing of her childhood, she describes herself as a little girl who was seemingly bright, good and bursting with health, who apparently deserved the appreciation of adults, but whose only real distinction was an unusual verbal fluency. She later came to recognize that her behaviour as a child had in part been hypocritical and designed to please, based as it was on the fear of rejection and loss of adult approval: drawing support from the admiration of her parents, she had secretly thought herself superior to other children. For all her success, an underlying anxiety associated with a sense of inadequacy and failure wrecked her capacity to mature happily.

The book tellingly describes the period of the onset of her anorexia, when euphoria appeared and masked the underlying depressive state. Through her hyper-activity, the girl felt alive and efficient; comparing herself with others, she felt them to be deplorably inefficient. To avoid dependence on her parents and on food, she nurtured the secret wish to become a person apart, remote from the world, a world that was experienced by her as increasingly disturbing. The book's protagonist points out several times that she had no awareness of suffering or of being ill, so that the question of treatment was either irrelevant or seen as an outright attack on her integrity and independence. Rather than something abnormal, the refusal of food was an extraordinary experience that enabled her to achieve a superior state of moral elevation. The patient saw her image, that of a completely flat and hollowed-out body, as a symbol of spiritual perfection. Just as Benvenuta was unaware that the attraction to the ascetic mental state was tantamount to an attraction to death, so the sense of omnipotence prevents an anorexic patient from seeing the danger of death as real. Asceticism and masochism are thus two faces of the same coin.

"Grant, O Lord, that I may become nothing!" was Simone Weil's heartfelt invocation (Raimbault & Eliacheff, 1989).

Simone Weil died in London on 24 August 1943, at the age of 34. Her death was due to the long series of privations to which she had voluntarily subjected herself and to her refusal to seek treatment for tuberculosis, aggravated by her state of malnutrition, after her failure to persuade the French authorities to agree to her plan for a corps of volunteer nurses to be parachuted into the bloodiest theatres of war, ready to die alongside the soldiers themselves. "A crazy project from the mind of a mad woman!" General de Gaulle is said to have commented.

In this way an indomitable intellectual died. A writer and philosopher, a restless and intransigent figure in France's trade union movement and in the French Marxist militant tendency between the wars, a convinced pacifist and supporter of the working class, Simone Weil shared the toil of the lowly and the exploited to the point of total physical exhaustion. She denied her body its fundamental needs, starved herself, scarcely covered herself with clothes, slept in the cold, carried on political activities, taught at a *lycée*, gave instruction to the workers, wrote articles and essays, and took part in the Spanish Civil War.

After a long series of failed attempts at political and social action, and at the height of an acute and profound intellectual crisis, she felt the intense presence of God. The writings of her last period are full of the experience of the divine: she believed in a strong and enlightening God who could convey the meaning of life.

However, that life was always a special life: "This world is uninhabitable; so one must flee into the other". Simone always did her utmost to achieve this, but exhaustion or illness limited her attempts to devote herself wholly to the cause and lose herself in others. Without her knowledge and, as usual, against her will, her parents intervened, but this time Simone managed to conceal her condition better and went under.

Her life had always been a confrontation with death. After a premature birth, at the age of six months she was wasting away

alarmingly because her sick mother insisted on continuing to breast-
feed her. After weaning, she fell ill. For five months she put on
hardly any weight and virtually ceased to grow; she did not walk
and refused to feed except from the bottle. She grew up in a family
environment characterized by a lack of affective response. The
mother, herself a brave and indomitable woman, discouraged any
manifestation of tenderness and femininity. At her instigation,
members of the family were forbidden to kiss or be kissed; physical
education and bodily activity enjoyed a privileged position, and
brilliant intellectual activity was valued in the children. On entering
the *lycée* at the age of 13, Simone lapsed into a severe depression
that made her contemplate suicide. She came out of this despair
with the intuition that she could emerge from the darkness by
making a continuous effort to penetrate into the realm of truth.
However, as we have seen, the wish for self-annihilation remained
the silent underlying passion of her life.

These life stories suggest the possible existence of a primal wish
for suffering and self-annihilation. This aspiration seems to bear out
Freud's hypothesis (in *Beyond the Pleasure Principle*, 1920g) of the
presence of a death drive at work inside us—a kind of primary
masochism which, when detached from the life drive and the self-
preservative wish, leads to death.

Deliberately avoiding any theoretical speculation, I have
adduced these dramatic biographies solely in order to illustrate a
kind of experience that could be called masochistic, in which the
exercise of spirituality can assume a self-destructive character. In the
name of the spiritual and the divine, a higher, sacrificial ideology
transforms the body into a theatre of suffering. The masochistic
urge, through the mystical union with the sacrificial body of God,
impels the subject towards a suffering similar in some respects to
the pleasure and exaltation of perversion.

A woman patient whose childhood had been filled with family
bereavements and agonizing separations spoke of a wound that
could not be healed: "It's the first thing I knew in life, and that can
end only when I plunge right inside it—so I shall end it with death
[...]. I don't know what this wound is, but it's an unbearable pain
and torture. You can never forget it, but you can't live with it either".

During the analysis an unexpected family drama threw her life
into confusion again, and once again the past was inexorably

repeated. The patient decided to break off the analysis. There followed a number of rage-filled sessions that culminated in a dream:

> While sitting beside a swimming pool I saw a girl fall over and hurt herself. A moment later a woman flung herself down from a trampoline, deliberately diving on to the marble pool surround. Even though her head was absolutely covered in clotted blood, the woman remained lucid, with her eyes open. I was worried about the girl who had fallen and asked some nurses who had meanwhile arrived how she was. Smiling, one of the nurses answered that she was dead.

It is all too easy to see that the blood clots on the head of the woman who had jumped from the trampoline represented the tormenting masochistic thoughts of death and self-destruction that had invaded the analytic space. Identified as she was with the woman who had plunged from the trampoline and smashed her head open, the patient showed herself to be partly terrified by and partly triumphant over the family drama that had once again taken possession of her affects, triggering her intention to break off the analysis. In the ensuing sessions, she painfully remembered that she really had injured herself on a marble staircase when she was four or five years old, at a particularly difficult time when she would dearly have loved to die.

The experience of Simone Weil and of certain traumatized patients seems to confirm that a masochistic attack on the subject's life may be a paradoxical response intended to silence the intolerable suffering of unbearable pain. The attack on the self can be seen as an attempt to blot out the feelings aroused by living in a desperate state of suffering.

The idealization of self-annihilation seems to result from an infantile pain that has never been worked through, resulting from prolonged and repeated traumatic experiences. Mute anger at the very fact of existing—rage at an implacable pain that has never been shared with anyone—breaks down the defences that were meant to ensure survival and sets the patient on the path towards death, which is idealized as a condition of absolute perfection and is pursued in a mental state of exaltation.

CHAPTER SEVEN

The clinical area of perversion

I n view of the extensive nature of the concept and the multiplicity of its components, as indicated by the large number of relevant clinical pictures and the voluminous contemporary psychoanalytic literature, the sadomasochistic perversion is difficult to define. It might, in fact, be better to speak of a multiplicity of sadomasochistic pictures, all differing from each other.

I shall now attempt to highlight certain clinical characteristics that will help us distinguish some areas of differing significance and severity.

Perversion and perverse–compulsive sexuality

A person who enjoys inflicting cruelty also likes to undergo it.

The Marquis de Sade, who has given his name to the aggressive side of perversion, sometimes likes to adopt the role of his victim. He is recorded as having asked to be flagellated or penetrated anally during the cyclic sexual excesses that laid him open to criminal prosecution. In "The one hundred and twenty days of

Sodom" (1784), the libertines enjoy undergoing the same tortures as they administer to the young people in their power.

Severin, the hero of Sacher-Masoch's *Venus in Furs* (1875), having enjoyed his masochistic pleasure, claims to be cured but then goes on to flog and torture women; in this way, he becomes the "hammer" instead of the "anvil".

Freud described the reversibility of the sadistic and masochistic positions with his customary clarity:

> A person who feels pleasure in producing pain in someone else in a sexual relationship is also capable of enjoying as pleasure any pain which he may himself derive from sexual relations. A sadist is always at the same time a masochist, although the active or the passive aspect of the perversion may be the more strongly developed in him and may represent his predominant sexual activity. [Freud, 1905d, p. 159]

The sadomasochistic perversion as described in this passage represents a constant form of sexual behaviour, which remains stable throughout life and whose roots lie in infancy. The clinical reality, however, is less straightforward: for perversion may appear sporadically and then disappear again, or it may be present alongside other, seemingly normal, sexual behaviours.

Glover (1933) notes that, during the psychotic crises observable in analyses, some patients have temporary perverse episodes, which serve for protection against anxieties that might trigger schizophrenic processes, thereby to some extent safeguarding the sense of reality. Glover attempts to extend this observation to all the perversions and hypothesizes a deeper perverse system that faithfully reflects the primal anxieties, so that the various perversions are seen to lie on a continuum extending from neuroses to psychoses.

Chasseguet-Smirgel (1992) stresses the importance of distinguishing both theoretically and clinically between (episodic) perverse behaviour and perversion as a structure.

Since individuals with structured sexual perversions have no perception of suffering and their perversions present themselves as an ego-syntonic search for pleasure, they seldom request help or therapy, unlike borderline patients who readily exhibit instances of perverse acting out in which suffering and anxiety are in the foreground.

It is surely not at all useful to liken compulsive perverse sexuality to sexual perversion, because this would obscure the important aetiological, structural and prognostic differences between these entities.

Perverse acting out, occurring at moments of crisis, has the function of defending against fear and anxiety, and operates by instantly changing the subject's mental state. Since the relief is only short-lived, the perverse act tends to be reproduced in every crisis situation.

The clinical symptomatology and the rapid appearance and disappearance of sexual acting out would seem to justify the theories of the Kohut and Winnicott schools, which see perverse sexuality as a defence against anxiety and the threat of the collapse of identity.

After a frustration that unleashes rage, the individual concerned enters into an excited mental state which impels him to engage in sexual encounters where he seeks triumph as compensation for humiliation or, conversely, a humiliation to punish himself masochistically. The acting out often takes a homosexual form, such as fellatio or passive anal penetration, frequently undertaken with transsexuals, who represent objects available for immediate acts of sexuality of a polymorphous type. One may wonder why these subjects engage in perverse acting out rather than in forms of "normal" sexuality.

Other forms of compulsive sexual behaviour traditionally classified as perversions, such as exhibitionism or some forms of transvestism, are also episodic and are associated with particular emotional factors, traumas or narcissistic wounds.

Impulsive behaviour is not rigorously structured like the stable perversions.

Patients who indulge in perverse acting out have polymorphous sexual relationships and display a variable potential for development; this contrasts with the stereotyped, rigid nature of a structured perversion, one of whose characteristics is that it does not oscillate between anxiety, rage and sexual excitation. I shall have more to say about this subject in connection with perverse defences in borderline structures.

The slide towards perversion may also represent an episodic defence against mental pain. Khan (1979) tells of a woman who met a man with whom she began, at his initiative, to practise a ritualized, masochistic type of sexuality. The sexual relationship continued for a while, until the woman succeeded in extricating herself from it. Even if this clinical account is presented as a case of perversion, the progress of the therapy shows that the perverse episode was the symptom of a concomitant depressive state; once the patient had overcome this, she was able to emerge from the masochistic relationship and from her passivity.

Feminine masochism of this kind is generally associated with depressive experiences or infantile deficiencies, and cannot be equated with the perverse structure. A particularly noteworthy point is that masochistic women never adopt a sadistic role, as is the case in structured perversions.

The two cases that follow illustrate different levels of organization and severity of the perversion. The first is a relatively minor instance which it was possible to work through, whereas the second was permanent and dramatic.

A very private case history

On 31 May 1922, at one of the famous Wednesday seminars of the Viennese Society, in the presence of Freud himself, the 27-year-old Anna Freud read her first scientific contribution, entitled "The relation of beating phantasies to a day-dream" (English version published 1923). Anna's aim was to be accepted as a practising analyst and be qualified to take part in psychoanalytic congresses.

Anna Freud notes in the written version of her lecture that the patient had undergone "a rather thoroughgoing analysis" (Young-Bruehl, 1988, p. 104), but does not say by whom. Since her paper was written six months before Anna took her first patient into therapy, it is quite likely that it actually constitutes a description of her own personal analysis, conducted by her father, Sigmund (ibid.). Freud left no written record of this analysis, but the material of one of the cases referred to in "A child is being beaten" (1919e) seems to refer to his daughter Anna. This paper is mentioned by Anna, who states that the emergence of beating fantasies in psychoanalytic treatments is much more frequent than might be supposed.

In the beating fantasy, persons who were once clearly identified have now been made unknown. The child being beaten is the same as the one fantasizing the masochistic scene, and the beating adult is the father. In the first version of the fantasy, a different child is beaten—a brother or sister competing for the father's love; this is a sexualized version of the Oedipus complex.

The originality of Anna Freud's account lies in the description of the psychic work performed by the little girl to distance herself from the masochistic fantasy and escape the sense of guilt. During the analysis, the significance of the fantasy is transformed and, while it remains a pleasing activity, it completely ceases to be connected with sadomasochistic pleasure. The girl becomes a deviser of tales and agreeable daydreams—the so-called nice stories—which are constantly renewed and ramified. Anna Freud demonstrates the kinship between the "nice stories" and the primitive beating fantasy, in which the protagonists are strong or weak, and adults and children contrast each other. In the "nice stories", the happy end is preceded by a period of anxiety and tension, followed by forgiveness and reconciliation and not by punishment: the fantasy and emotion are separated from the sexual component, and the content of the fantasy changes.

The "nice stories" therefore appear as a successful attempt at sublimation of the unconscious incestuous fantasies and of the Oedipal rivalries that were initially placed on an anal–sadistic level.

A tragic and exemplary tale

The protagonist here is Yukio Mishima, whose life ended in terrible circumstances, as foreshadowed in his autobiographical tale *Confessions of a Mask* (1960), written when he was 22. Mishima took his own life at the age of 45, on the day when he finished the last novel in his tetralogy *The Sea of Fertility*, a masterpiece that brought him worldwide fame. On 25 November 1970, after kidnapping a general and attempting to harangue the troops, the writer committed *hara-kiri* with a sword and had himself beheaded by a follower. In her brilliant study *Mishima, a Vision of the Void*, Marguerite Yourcenar (1980) sees his entire literary oeuvre as dedicated to death and his death by his own hand as the last of his works. Whereas death appears as the final act of his delusional, cruel anxiety, the testimony of the autobiographical account of his youth, *Confessions of a Mask* (1960), restores Mishima to us as a much more human but at the same time enigmatic character. The mask he must wear serves to deny his irreducible differentness, both to others and, to a certain extent, to himself too.

As a child, he was taken away from his mother by an awful grandmother, who transferred him to her own apartment. Mishima thus grew up with an ailing old woman, permanently shut up in a suffocatingly malodorous room until he himself periodically fell ill with diseases that all but carried him off.

The vision that both fascinated and tormented him appeared when, at the age of four, he saw "someone coming down the slope" (Mishima, 1960, p. 11f.): it was a handsome, muscular young man, carrying a yoke of night-soil buckets, a nightsoilman with a filthy sweatband round his head and wearing torn "thigh-puller" trousers. The protagonist then had a presentiment of "a kind of desire like stinging pain": looking up at this dirty youth, he felt choked by desire and thought he would like to become him. His desire had two focal points: the young man's dark-blue "thigh-pullers", and his occupation. He felt "something like a yearning for a piercing pain, a body-wrenching sorrow". All these sensations bore down on him and took him captive.

Among the images in the many picture books with which he spent his solitary childhood, one figure captured his fancy and transported him to a dream-like world (*ibid.*, p. 13). Whenever he reached this page, "his heart would beat fast". The picture showed a knight mounted on a white horse, brandishing his drawn sword against a blue sky, confronting some hurtling object full of evil power. The knight would surely die on the following page, and the tumultuous throbbing of the little reader's heart accompanied the anticipation of his death. Mishima's tale is a meticulous account of the infantile fantasies surrounding literary characters, stories whose happy ending was changed into a grim dénouement, representations or drawings of young *samurai* with their chests ripped open or strapping, sweaty fighters. Adolescence opened the door to the pleasure of sexuality, kindled by the sight of the young, tortured body of Guido Reni's St Sebastian, his lips distorted with melancholic pleasure. Yet in the book there is also the suggestion of a possible relationship with the sensitive girl Sonoko, whom the

*perverse structure is not
object related or about
conflict + anx*

hero approaches uncertainly and timorously like any adolescent; he studies her movements with a view to getting close to her and achieving physical contact—a kiss—thus potentially paving the way to a world in which relating is possible. But mere wishing does not open the door to this other reality, for which he is not cut out; the young man remains numb and, keeping his mask on, runs away from the love he has nevertheless succeeded in arousing.

Years later the two meet by chance; Sonoko has since married and he has grown more adult. The drama that threatens him is now more acute and painful. The presence of Sonoko again offers itself as an area of serenity that is doomed to vanish. The pair meet at a popular dance hall and compare notes on their lives. Suddenly Mishima's eye is caught by a group of youths. One of them has taken off his shirt and "stood there half-naked, rewinding a belly-band about his middle" (*ibid.*, p. 171). This impresses Mishima, and Sonoko's existence is forgotten:

> I was thinking of but one thing: Of his going out onto the streets of high summer just as he was, half-naked, and getting into a fight with a rival gang. Of a sharp dagger cutting through that belly-band, piercing that torso. Of that soiled belly-band beautifully dyed with blood. Of his gory corpse being put on an improvised stretcher, made of a window shutter, and brought back here ... [*ibid.*, p. 172]

These two paradigm cases reflect the complexity of the clinical phenomenology of perversion.

Whereas Anna Freud's infantile beating fantasy is connected with the Oedipal conflict, the obliteration of aggression and the exaltation of the victim state,[1] Mishima's case belongs to the malign variety of the perverse experience, manifested as a hypnotic power to which the resigned protagonist submits.

In this case the infantile fantasy underlies the fascination of death, acted out and suffered in the sexualized male body. The ecstatic attraction makes the outcome irreparable. There are no Oedipal problems or sibling rivalries to be circumvented and overcome. The excitement aroused by suffering and the idealization of sacrifice, firmly ensconced early on in the infantile imagination, preclude any possibility of becoming a partner in a love relationship. The apotheosis of martyrdom (the St Sebastian who is loved so melancholically and erotically) ultimately will be attained personally.

Note

1. The infantile beating fantasy was quite a common symptom in past decades; I do not know if it is still as frequent today. Apart from Anna Freud, sufferers included Lou Andreas-Salomé and Sabina Spielrein, an analysand of Jung's with whom he had an affair. It is my impression that this symptom was not unconnected with the type of upbringing prevailing at the time, an integral part of which was corporal punishment, administered by the parents (often the father). Seen in this light, the symptom is a compulsion to repeat and erotize the trauma. .

CHAPTER EIGHT

Theories of sadomasochistic perversion

"The advance of science is not comparable to the changes of a
city, where old edifices are pitilessly torn down to give place to
new, but to the continuous evolution of zoologic types which
develop ceaselessly and end by becoming unrecognizable to
the common sight, but where an expert eye finds always traces
of the prior work of centuries past. One must not think then
that the old-fashioned theories have been sterile and vain"

Poincaré, 1982, p. 208

oday's psychoanalysts, unlike those of the past, do not see
themselves as members of rival élites each claiming to be in
sole possession of the truth; they have learned to coexist and
to tone down the intensity of the debate and of their ideological
controversies. For this reason, the various movements and the
associated theories, while clearly distinguishing themselves from
one another, stand in a relationship of contiguity, pursuing different
routes towards understanding the reality they seek to investigate.

Confining the field to a single sexual perversion, sadomasochism,
I shall attempt to show that a number of different theoretical
viewpoints on this subject coexist in psychoanalysis.

Every theory entails a model that facilitates understanding of the object of its study, while at the same time inhibiting possible vital new approaches to problematic and unknown aspects. Moreover, no theory is exhaustive: while a theory may seem to grasp something important about perversion, ultimately it merely emphasizes some facets while neglecting others (Barale & Ferruta, 1997).

The Freudian model, for all its complexity and intricate structure, is an oversimplification, in that it situates all perversions —including homosexuality—within the sphere of the drive.

Other theories have followed, some of which, while by no means supplanting or superseding Freud's construction, have intertwined with it.

Notwithstanding the central position occupied by sexuality in psychoanalysis, its interpretation is not at all univocal, and the same is true of perversion. The inter-relationship between the various psychoanalytic standpoints is complex, in accordance with the different and mutually complementary theories that underlie them.

After the discovery of infantile sexuality, Freud held that a person's growth proceeded in parallel with sexual maturation; he identified the various phases of this maturation, which constituted the psychosexual development of the individual. Later psychoanalytic research led to different results and theories, which have added to and completed the model. For some authors, sexuality and psychic development proceed along separate pathways: in their view, the processes of introjection and identification necessary for growth take place without the involvement of sexual fantasy, so that for them psycho-emotional development follows a different route from infantile sexuality.

Studies on the subject of sexuality are still current in psycho-analysis, as the contemporary debate on gender identity shows. Many aspects of personality connected with sexuality and the erotic imagination (for instance, the choice of love object or the roots of sexual identity) have not yet been sufficiently clarified.

In a paper published in 1956, Balint considers two possible approaches to perversion. The first, which refers to Freud's theory of the component drives and various organizations of the libido, links perversion to infantile forms of sexuality. In Balint's view, major problems with this first type of definition are presented both by homosexuality (if seen as a perversion) and by sadomasochism (which cannot readily be deemed an infantile phase of psychosexual development). The second approach, based on object-relations theory, emphasizes the difference between genital love and perversion and notes in particular that any form of love for a human object is lacking in perversion.

In view of the difficulty of establishing a single common denominator for its various forms, some contemporary authors prefer not to regard perversion as a single whole. Kernberg (1992), for example, considers that the perversions should not be seen as a psychopathological entity in their own right, but instead be classified in accordance with the subject's type of personality organization—neurotic, borderline, narcissistic or psychotic.

Current psychoanalytic theories can be divided into three groups, each with its own fundamental position.

1. In the first group of theories, which may be called *the first paradigm*, the sadomasochistic perversion is regarded as a deviation in sexual behaviour, and the emphasis is placed on a disturbance of sexuality. These theories espouse Freud's hypotheses on infantile sexuality and the role of sexuality. The psychosexual model, which faithfully conforms to Freud's descriptions, sees perversion as a section through, and crystallization of, the libidinal and aggressive tensions that characterize the development of human sexuality. Chasseguet-Smirgel is the most modern and consistent protagonist of this theoretical perspective.

2. The second group, or *second paradigm*, comprises the relational theories. These stress the defensive function of sexuality, and deem the anxieties that threaten personal identity to be central to the understanding of perversion. This position is adopted by authors such as Khan, who owe allegiance to the thought of Winnicott, and others, such as the American analysts, who subscribe to Kohut's theories. Kohut saw perversion as a narcissistic object relationship, potentially directed towards sounder forms of structuring of the self.

3. Other schools, inspired by the work of Klein, which constitute my *third paradigm*, consider perversion to be a sexualization of power and cruelty—a psychopathological structure of the personality. Sexual love, which brings about the union of pleasure and of concern for the object, is distinguished from perverse excitation, which arises out of triumph over the other and the pleasure of

destruction. Cruelty plays a pre-eminent part, and sexuality is a fulfilment, a sexualized triumph. The principal authors represented in this approach are Meltzer and Rosenfeld.

Whereas the libido theory sees sexuality as a complex phenomenon, an unconscious force that enters into complicated relational vicissitudes and often fails to reach its natural outlet, which ought to coincide with genital love, relational theories refer to the traditional conception of sexuality as pleasure or excitation in the sexual relationship. This pleasure is seen as having an integrating and defensive function with respect to anxiety. The erotized defence (the erotic form of mania, as Winnicott once described it) is directed mainly against the mental pain resulting from object loss, rage and the sense of guilt.

The British school that followed Klein (Rosenfeld, Meltzer and Joseph), for its part, does not inquire into the nature of sexuality in itself, but focuses on the object relationship and the constructive or destructive orientation of the personality and its internal objects.

Whereas for Freud it is sexuality that organizes the psyche, for Klein it is the other way round. Sexuality, as an expression of the internal world, is perverse only when the components directed towards power and the devaluation of the object gain the upper hand. Children, in the Kleinian and post-Kleinian theory, are motivated by love or by destructive hate; the predominance of one or other of these two positions will be decisive for the orientation of their sexuality.

As this outline shows, present-day psychoanalytic approaches to sexual perversion reflect both the development of psychoanalytic theory and the models corresponding to the various theories represented in contemporary thought. We see that the drive model and the Oedipus complex have given way to the structural model; the theory of object relations to the conflict between libidinal and destructive aspects of the personality; and the vicissitudes of the process of separation–individuation to the structuring of the self.

I shall now attempt to describe the three paradigms, and to show how the different approaches complement each other.

Psychosexuality

Freud's capacity to formulate increasingly complex theories of the psychical apparatus to complement those that prove incomplete is one of the strengths of his thought. To understand how perversion was conceptualized, the following brief sketch of the transformations undergone by the concept of sexuality during the course of Freud's elaboration of metapsychology will be useful.

Three periods can be distinguished in Freud's oeuvre, in which he presented three models of the psychical apparatus, and which partly correspond to three successive theoretical views of sexuality.

In the *first period*, which ends with *Studies on Hysteria* (1895d [1893–1895]), Freud identifies sexuality as the pathogenic agent of neurosis, which he theorized as having a traumatic aetiology (this conception was revised later), and which he divided into the actual neuroses, attributed to an accumulation of undischarged sexual excitation, and the psychoneuroses. The sexuality referred to in this theory is that of conventional language, of repressed sexual and love-related desire.

In the *second period*, the aetiological hypothesis of neurosis coincides with a general theory of individual development. Sexuality is now seen not in its ordinary sense of sexual love, but in a "psychoanalytic"—i.e. metaphorical and metapsychological— sense, which allows perversion to be interpreted. The sexuality described in *Three Essays on the Theory of Sexuality* (1905d) results from the modification of two kinds of parameters; the first concerns the extent and sphere of sexuality, while the second involves a qualitative and conceptual transformation.

Libido theory, in accordance with the primacy of the pleasure principle, extends the range of sexuality so that it includes all forms of bodily pleasure. All sensory forms of pleasure are seen as primitive components of libido; even the infant's sensory pleasure in sucking constitutes an expression of sexuality.

Sexuality remains closely bound up with the energy model. Freud (1909d) explains that, in obsessional neurosis, the process of thought itself may be sexualized, and a repetitive sequence of ideas may be experienced as a substitute for sexual pleasure. When psychotics, such as Senatspräsident Schreber (Freud, 1911), are unable to cope with the large quantity of drive energy released in their illness, part of this energy is sexualized. Freud describes this process in terms of the hydraulic metaphor of a liquid that overflows from a vessel and can be neither contained nor neutralized.

Perverse sexuality is nothing but one of the variants of sexuality;

it results from the distortion of libidinal development and the maturation of the ego, and arises out of difficulty in overcoming the normal stages of libidinal organization. The pervert in consequence remains locked into a pregenital sexuality.

The *third period* begins with the turning point of 1920: sexuality, contrasted with the destructive drive, is now deemed to coincide with the positive force of love, holding the two together and opposing destruction. Sexuality is no longer a primitive, aggressive force, the perverse–polymorphous component drive, but Eros engaged in a continuous battle with Thanatos.

It is important to note that, in the progressive modulation of Freud's theory, sexuality is always conceived as unitary: it varies in its expression, has aggressive or affectionate components, can bind, unite and oppose the destructive instinct, but always remains within a unitary model.

The first paradigm

The psychosexual theory

The first paradigm coincides with the theories that followed Freud's discoveries concerning infantile sexuality.

The declared intention of the *Three Essays on the Theory of Sexuality* (1905d) is to study the sexual drive, its energy, aim and object. Taking sexual perversions as his starting point, Freud describes infantile sexuality and its transformations at puberty, and regards neurotic symptoms as a disturbance of sexuality. The perversions, too, are held to be fixations and regressions to the perverse, polymorphous sexuality of the child.

The choice of sexual object is variable and determined by a large number of factors, both constitutional and accidental, which explain the multiplicity of outcomes. It is the sexual drive that makes for the plurality of variations and degradations of the object, since this drive is originally independent of the object. The aims of the drive can bring about all the intermediate relations with the sexual object before coitus. Perversion is seen as a fixation to, and replacement of, the normal aim by intermediate aims already present in the normal sexual process.

The key concepts here are: (1) deviations in respect of the object; (2) deviations in respect of the aim; (3) the bisexual predisposition;

and (4) the idealization of the drive.

In particular, for example in fetishism, since there is an overvaluation of the object, the sexual aim is relinquished. The loss of the normal aim of the wish is attributed to an infantile trauma resulting in an attempt to find a substitute, or to early sexual stimulation. The link with normality is the overvaluation of the loved object, which is connected with the degree of fetishism characteristic of love, or, rather, of the state of being in love.

The hypothesis is that the drive is made up of a set of different elements, each of which, when activated, is responsible for a different perversion.

Freud notes that most people's sexuality always seems to be mixed with a dose of aggression and a tendency towards oppression. In sadism and masochism, the link with normality is stated to be constituted by the aggressive component of the drive, which makes itself independent and is hypertrophied. Neurotic symptoms stem not only from the normal sexual drive but also from perverse components, and neurosis is seen as the negative of perversion, in that symptoms represent the conversion of perverse drives. In neurotic patients, sexual life begins in the same way as that of the future pervert, involving a childhood replete with polymorphous sexual activity that is subsequently neutralized by repression.

Infantile sexuality is based on the vital functions and, since the component drives do not necessarily need a sexual object, the aim may be an erogenic zone of the body. Fore-pleasure is obtained by excitation, while end-pleasure leads to satisfaction. Through fore-pleasure, the erogenic zones permit the production of the pleasure of satisfaction. Perversion is when the preparatory action substitutes for the sexual aim.

Some component drives (looking, exhibiting, or cruelty), on the other hand, call from the beginning for other persons as sexual objects. Object choice takes place in two stages, separated by the latency period, which paves the way for the development of affection in a relationship. At puberty, the infantile objects must be given up and the development of the sexual current resumed.

Owing to the diachrony of object choice, the object is rediscovered at puberty. Whereas in the infant sexual satisfaction was autoerotic and bound up with the ingestion of food, after puberty the libido will be object-related.

Psychosexual development is substantially determined both by constitutional elements (the strength of the drive, of repression and of reaction formation) and by environmental factors. These two groups are linked in a compensatory relationship, the "complemental series", whereby a diminution in the intensity of one factor is offset by an increase in that of the other. Important determinants of perversions prove to be fixations to impressions from the infantile period, the adhesiveness of memory traces of pregenital sexuality, and spontaneous sexual precocity that interrupts the latency period.

Among the perversions, sadism and masochism occupy a particular position. The pleasure derived from cruelty—that is, sadism—stems from infantile sexuality and dominates the pregenital organization. Cruelty is a spontaneous manifestation in the child's character; conversely, the inhibition of the drive of appropriation and the capacity for compassion with the suffering of pain are of relatively late onset.

The infant-specific absence of the compassion barrier carries the risk that the link between cruel drives and erotic drives will become unbreakable in later life. The pair of opposites constituted by activity/passivity, which belongs to the generality of sexual life, is present in characteristic fashion; the particularity of the sadomasochistic perversion lies in the fact that the active and passive forms are encountered in one and the same person.

In "Instincts and their vicissitudes" (1915c), Freud reinforces the hypothesis of pairs of opposites and suggests that transformation into the opposite is one of the aims of the drive. The passive aim becomes established in the place of the active one, and sadism is transformed into masochism.

Another mechanism at work here is turning back on the subject's own person. The sadomasochistic perversion is thus described as becoming established in two stages: first the child derives pleasure from a sadistic fantasy, and later the same sadistic act is imagined and experienced as being inflicted on himself.

In "A child is being beaten" (1919e), perversion is attributed primarily to the Oedipus complex, incestuous love for the father, and sibling rivalry. The triumph or pleasure in imagining a child being beaten stems from the satisfaction of seeing an Oedipal rival humiliated. Perverse satisfaction is the aborted fruit of a phase of libidinal development. The perversion not only expresses the persistence of the component impulse but also results from an inability to overcome the Oedipal position. From this point of view, both the (ego-dystonic) neurotic symptom and the (ego-syntonic) perverse symptom represent the residue of the overall process of development of infantile sexuality (De Martis, 1989).

Freud reconstructs the sequence whereby the sadomasochistic fantasy arises. The first exciting image ("my father is beating the child") is the sight of the father beating a hated child, the rival. The beating fantasy is an attempt to avoid the Oedipal conflict: out of the negative feelings of rage and despair, the child constructs the sadistic scene in which the rival is beaten and publicly humiliated. In this first phase, the fantasy, which is still sexualized, serves to obliterate the bond of love between the father and another child.

The second image ("I am being beaten by my father"), on the other hand, represents the fulfilment of sexual love for the father, obtained by masochistic submission. The reversal of the fantasy from "sadistic" into "masochistic" is only apparent: the child, even if she is being beaten, wants to be the father's only love object and to have children by him.

"An adult is beating a child" (no longer the father, but a stranger): this becomes the third fantasy capable of inducing orgasm. The first two fantasies are unconscious, and only the latter belongs to consciousness.

Freud constantly emphasizes the role of the Oedipus complex in the progressive development of the fantasy, which is merely aggressive in the first part and is sexualized only subsequently. In the masochistic version, it represents a regressive derivative of incestuous love. The perversion not only expresses the persistence of the component impulse, but also results from an incapacity to overcome the Oedipal position.

The conscious fantasy of the adult beating a child appears in consequence of the stimulation of reality, such as witnessing a scene of corporal punishment, or of reading books. Its development shows the operation of memory in the perverse fantasy. Freud assigns a complex position to memory, which does not record facts but constructs its own images *a posteriori* by deferred action in a process of continuous transformation. Hence the occurrence of actual beating is of little moment. The concept of deferred action shows the importance of the transforming work of memory, which changes both internal and external reality (Novick & Novick, 1996, 1997).

Freud's theoretical work was built upon during those years by an important contribution from one of his pupils, Sachs ("On the genesis of the perversions", 1923 [1986]), who contends that perverse pleasure represents the persistence in consciousness of a fragment of infantile experience. This experience acquires a particular link to the ego, so that it is preserved unchanged through all the ensuing transformations. The ego cannot get rid of it; the compromise is similar to that arising in a neurotic symptom and consists in the displacement of a part of infantile sexuality into the repressive system. In this way the ego succeeds in partially controlling the pregenital drive, albeit at the expense of its own strength. In Sachs's view, Freud's statement that neurosis is the "negative" of perversion is not all there is to the matter, because perversion is only the conscious aspect of a larger unconscious system. Sachs makes an interesting comparison between simple perversions, in which the sexual fantasy arises in ego-syntonic form, and complex ones, in which neurotic phobia and perverse satisfactions alternate.

To sum up, the drive theory postulates the following (Gillespie, 1956):

(1) Sexual perversion in adulthood is based on the same components as those that make up infantile sexuality.
(2) Only one or two tendencies of the polymorphism of infantile sexuality are reproduced in perversion.
(3) Perversion is a form of defence against castration anxiety, which makes it impossible for the subject to confront and successfully overcome the Oedipus complex.
(4) This form of defence entails a regression of the libido to the pregenital level, where the sadistic component is present to a greater degree. Anxiety and the sense of guilt are "libidinized".
(5) In perversion, the ego simultaneously accepts both the primitive drive and the defence, and grants them a limited outlet. This compromise is obtained at the cost of a permanent split in the ego and of a partial disavowal of reality.

Freud's theoretical leap dates from the 1920s, when he replaced the single-drive theory by the dual theory of the drives. In "The economic problem of masochism" (1924c), Freud developed a number of ideas that opened up new perspectives.

The new dual drive theory overcomes an ambiguity inherent in the libido theory, namely that sadism and masochism contradict the hypothesis of the primacy of the pleasure principle and of the avoidance of suffering. If the hypothesis of the death drive is accepted, the aggression inherent in sadomasochism takes on a different meaning: sadomasochistic pleasure is no longer identified with the excitation of possessing, dominating and controlling the sexual love object described in the libido theory.

The sadomasochistic perversion is not a simple epiphenomenon of infantile sexuality, but results from the fusion of the two drives, the life drive and the death drive. The concept of the fusion of the drives becomes the theoretical cornerstone of the new vision: the two drives cannot remain free, for if they did, the drive would be dangerously capable of wreaking destruction.

Primary masochism, instead of being governed by the pleasure principle, is interpreted in the light of the Nirvana principle, the pleasure of self-annihilation. The hypothesis of the death drive calls into question the possible existence of a primal masochism not derived from the reversal of sadism.

Freud maintained for a long time that there was no such thing as a primary masochism and that masochism was nothing but sadism turned upside-down: the masochist was a masochist because he wished to assume the role of victim, reversing his position as a sadist. In "The economic problem of masochism", however, Freud contends that masochism is primary, and therefore neither complementary nor secondary to sadism. Masochism is now a transformation of the destructive impulse, which is turned against the subject's own self.

Whereas in 1919 Freud explained masochism as a convergence of the sense of guilt and sexual love, leading to the fantasy of being beaten by the father, he now contends that part of the destructive drive is not used as such but remains inside the individual, bound to the libido through sexual excitation, and thus becomes transformed into primary erotogenic masochism.

The concepts used by Freud in this paper open the way to the interpretation of moral masochism. In showing that sexual masochism has a counterpart in the moral field, and that morality can be distorted in the direction of self-aggression, he demonstrates his familiarity with the death drive. In moral masochism, the intimidatory character of morality brings about the punishment of the guilty party. However, being treated as guilty is not the same thing as feeling guilty. The masochist admits his guilt and demands punishment in order to enjoy the pleasure of aggression against his self; the moral aspect, which at first sight seems to conceal guilt feelings, in fact reveals the pleasure of punishment.

Besides erotogenic and moral masochism, Freud describes feminine masochism. In his psychosexual theory, female sexuality takes on a derogatory connotation: "feminine" indicates passivity and coincides with the passive aim of the drive. This term first appears when Freud refers to the theory of sexual trauma as the aetiological factor in hysteria (Davis, 1993). On the basis of the idea that "anatomy is destiny", Freud equates the feminine position with the passive receptivity of the vagina receiving the penis during sexual intercourse, the male organ being seen as performing the active, penetrating role.

The narcissistic aim is associated with the "feminine" attitude, whether it appears in a woman (hysteria) or in a man (homosexuality and paranoia), through the inversion of the Oedipus complex.

We have already considered Freud's description of the Wolf Man's erotized position of submission to his father. Freud later (1931b) continues to stress women's tendency—both cultural and constitutional—to suppress aggression and to develop masochistic tendencies. The idea, borrowed from Krafft-Ebing, that masochism is a feminine prerogative and that male masochism reflects feminine aspects, has proved very tenacious.

Freud's ideas on masochism are thus seen to be highly variegated and complex: masochism emerges as a variable in the aim of the sexual drive, a mental characteristic and a distorted form of object relationship.

Freud's last contribution on perversion is the brief paper "Fetishism" (1927e), in which he considers the importance of the splitting of the ego.

Its central thesis is that fetishism stems from the inability to overcome castration anxiety. The fetish represents the persistence of the belief that women have a penis—a belief whose function is to reassure the subject and thereby keep castration anxiety at bay. The fetishistic objects are ones to be captured by the eyes: unconsciously, the fetishist is always out to catch sight of the female genitals. The foot or shoe, fur (suggestive of pubic hair) or women's underclothing all stand for the female sexual organ. The fetish, the female phallus, reassures the fetishist, mitigating the anxiety that he might be castrated.

The belief in the existence of the female phallus involves a non-recognition of reality and a double truth: on the one hand, the fetishist accepts the absence of the penis, and on the other he disavows it. This double reality is made possible only by a splitting of the ego, the result of which is the fetish.

Present-day drive theories

Swinging as it does between the theory of the component drive and the new conception of drive duality, Freud's interpretation of perversion leaves a wide margin of uncertainty and lends itself to opposing explanations.

Freud's contributions never follow a univocal course; older formulations are often not clearly integrated into subsequent ones. Such a position is inevitable with a method like that of psycho-analysis, which constantly develops and broadens the field of knowledge. This is an expression of the need to keep the investigative pathway open and not to block it by an excessively limiting, univocal conceptualization. However, some contradictions can perhaps not be resolved dialectically.

Conceptualizations with contrasting, multiple meanings, recast at different periods of theoretical investigation, also have some disadvantages (Sandler, Holder, Dare & Dreher, 1997). They result in divergent areas of theoretical elaboration, which Freud's successors have attempted to reconcile. Freud never repudiated the edifice of the libidinal drives even after he had indirectly abandoned it in favour of the death drive.

The unresolved issue is whether the sadomasochistic perversion is characterized by the infantile aspects of sexuality, as the drive theory maintains, or should be seen as an expression of the death drive, albeit mitigated by sexuality, as the dual drive theory suggests.

Analysts are divided on this question. For some, who have remained faithful to the psychosexual theory, the single libidinal drive has remained the interpretative parameter for perversion (Paradigm 1). Others, by contrast, have proceeded from the hypothesis of the existence of both the libidinal drive and the death drive (Paradigm 3).

One answer to the questions left unresolved by Freud is given by

Chasseguet-Smirgel (1985, 1986), the author of a consistent, well-documented theory, whose key points are: (a) regressive anality; (b) disavowal of the differences between the sexes and the generations; and (c) the role of splitting.

Chasseguet-Smirgel attempts to combine Freud's pre- and post-1920 conceptions within a single theoretical structure, and to integrate the psychosexual theory, together with the various levels of libidinal development and the associated points of regression, with the theory of the death drive. In the pervert, owing to excessive castration anxiety, the path to the development of a genital object relationship is blocked, and its place is taken by a sexuality dominated by the faecal phallus. The result is the creation of an anal world in which there is no awareness of the difference between the sexes and the generations.

Whereas in normal development the ego ideal, projected on to the figure of the Oedipal father, promotes a healthy resolution of the Oedipus complex, in the perverse case the pregenital drives are idealized. The mother is decisive because of her massive cathexis of her child, who is considered as a phallus. In this way the child grows up in the illusion of being a "husband–child" for her. The mother is unable, and (unconsciously) unwilling, to allow her child to emerge from symbiosis and to help him acquire an independent identity. Instead, she encourages him to deny the role of the father in the primal scene and to obliterate the genital universe of procreation, replacing it with the pregenital dimension, which is the only one accessible to the child.

The equation of penis–faeces–child is taken literally by the pervert, who, by denying genitality and establishing an anal universe, can bridge the gap between child and adult and deny the difference between the sexes, between the generations and between mother and child. Perversion thus comes to be seen as superior to any other form of pleasure or love relationship.

A splitting mechanism (Freud, 1927e) allows the perverse world to exist alongside the real world, so that limited psychotic functioning becomes possible. The pervert knows up to a point that faeces are not equivalent to the father's penis, but at the same time he does not know this, encouraged as he is in this ignorance by the mother. The pervert has suffered not from a narcissistic deficiency but rather from an excess of narcissistic cathexis, the sudden disappearance of which may prove unbearable.

In Chasseguet-Smirgel's first theory, perversion is regarded as a regression to the anal–sadistic stage of development. In her later writings, however, this regression is characterized differently: it is no longer a regression to an anal–sadistic universe, but instead to a uterine world in which the pleasure principle coincides with the death drive. This return proceeds back-wards along the route from homogeneity to heterogeneity and represents a victory of the pleasure principle over the reality principle.

The nucleus of perversion is described in a patient's dream:

> A fish is exhibited with its mouth open. You can see the inside of the body, which is smooth. We bet that we can throw a pebble into its mouth, and that it will roll right down to the anus and come out. Then the fish's mouth puckers up and changes into a vagina. It retracts. The vagina and the anus are now one and the same thing. Then it becomes something like a snake-penis. Right beside, there is an exhibition about the Jewish people. There stands X, toward whom I feel homosexually attracted. From time to time, people have to climb up onto stepladders. In fact, we are in a gas chamber. [Chasseguet-Smirgel, 1986, p. 82]

The hollow inside of the fish, so utterly smooth, stands for the interior of the maternal uterus, which no longer presents any obstacle—a mother's womb in which the subject can do anything he likes. It is a fatherless universe, in which the subject, by "anal production", attributes to himself the powers of the Creator.

In my opinion, however, Chasseguet-Smirgel fails to connect the representation of the extermination camp with the logical consequence of the development of perverse pleasure. The pleasure of dominating the object becomes the legitimacy of annihilating a defenceless victim, as in a Nazi concentration camp. The pleasure of transgression, the dream seems to suggest, places perversion in the sphere of criminality.

An eclectic attempt at synthesis, falling within the first paradigm, is made by Kernberg (1992), who correctly emphasizes the importance of the level of organization of the personality whereby the perversion is maintained, and identifies three relevant groups.

The first is the neurotic group; the second, of intermediate severity, comprises the borderline and narcissistic personality; and the third corresponds to malignant narcissism, the antisocial personality and psychosis. According to Kernberg, perversion, when present on the neurotic level, depends on distortion of the impulse and on the libidinal conflict. Borderline personalities exhibit a condensation of Oedipal and pre-Oedipal conflicts with an excess of pre-Oedipal aggression. Only perversions of the narcissistic structures show the dynamic constellation of the regressive anal universe described by Chasseguet-Smirgel (Kernberg, 1991). These are cases of intolerance of reality, coupled with denial of the difference between the sexes and generations.

Perversions of the neurotic structure are distinguished from those of the borderline personality, but the greatest differences are observed in the antisocial personality, in which aggression is unbridled and the superego functions are damaged.

The second paradigm

Post-Kohutian and post-Winnicottian relational theories

I shall cite some of the many authors who consider the structuring role of sexuality to be fundamental to the development of the self and to the acquisition of identity, and who have thereby opened the way to relational theories of the perversions.

Winnicott (1945) contends that only an appropriate, sensual way of being held by the mother can give the child the perception of an entity contained within the surface of the body.

Greenacre (1958) stresses the importance of the first psychosexual experiences—in particular, those concerning the genitals—in establishing the sense of sexual and personal identity.

Spitz (1959) holds that the psychosexual experiences, fantasies or sexual acts of early infancy constitute psychic organizers directed towards normal consolidation of the self and the representation of objects.

Mahler (Mahler, Pine, & Bergman, 1975) postulates that the child arrives at a primitive body image through the instinctualization of the body surface resulting from pleasurable sexual contacts with the mother.

According to Kohut (1971), the child's primitive voyeuristic and exhibitionistic relationship, combining with an appropriate maternal response, undergoes a gradual transformation: an archaic narcissistic configuration gives way to a sense of self-esteem, cohesion and continuity of the self. Kohut (1977) hypothesizes that some adult patients with narcissistic personalities must, in infancy, have had to face the isolation and depression caused by an absent or unempathic self-object (the parents) and to sustain themselves with masturbatory activities. The sexualized wishes express a need to incorporate the missing object and to reassure the self that it is alive and whole.

The theoretical contributions of the authors in this paradigm are decidedly original. Child development is no longer determined by drive forces but takes place by a complex process of interaction between subject and environment; the biological substrate is transformed into a relational matrix. The lack of an average expectable environment represents a betrayal by the world, causing the child to regress to a narcissistic state in which sensory and illusionary modalities of support and survival predominate.

The analogies with drive theory are apparent only, since the component drives, with the associated phases of development and points of fixation to various levels, are also abandoned here.

According to Kohut (1996), the perversions cannot be approached by placing them in the context of the psychology of the pregenital drives, which nevertheless explains a great deal. In Kohut's view, perversion is something more than, and different from, the simple domination of the pregenital component drives. The perversions call for the consideration of a wide range of aspects of the personality if the intense and irresistible dependence on pleasure is to be explained.

Kohut (1977, p. 128) associates the intensity of pleasure with the structural deficiency and lack of integration of the self. The behavioural manifestations of perversion are, in his view, a secondary phenomena:

> After a break-up of the primary psychological unit (assertively demanded empathy-merger with the self-object), the drive appears as a disintegration product; the drive is then enlisted in the attempt to bring about the lost merger (and thus the repair of the self) by pathological means, i.e. as enacted in the fantasies and actions of the pervert. [*ibid.*]

Similarly, in the relational theories inspired by Kohut, sexual experience coincides with erotic infantile pleasure, affording a partial defence against evacuation of the self when the child constantly lacks an average expectable environment.

The innovation in this approach is that the perversions are seen as sexualized attempts to avoid experiences of psychic death or fragmentation. They can thus be linked to Glover's (1933) prior intuitions of perversion as a defence against psychotic anxieties.

Analysts of the Kohut school derive their interpretation of perversion from the fact that erotic experience gives rise to a state of grandiosity of the self that is necessary for the structuring and cohesion of the child's sense of identity. In their view, sexuality and sexual pleasure do not merely defend against anxiety but also have a restructuring and reparative function.

An apt summing-up of this theory is presented by Stolorow (1979), who demonstrates the importance of the role attributed to "sexuality" in the genesis of the perversions. Whenever the individual experiences an injury to or breakdown of a grandiose–narcissistic psychic attitude, he returns to the archaic experience of sexualization; this also occurs during psychoanalytic treatment.

More complex perversions are interpreted in the same way: the orgasm of the masochist, who assumes the role of a victim, is seen as an attempt to re-establish the perception of existing through pain and submission, thus allowing a grandiose identification with the sadistic partner.

Khan (1979), a member of the British Independent Group owing allegiance to Winnicott's thought, develops a similar approach to the one just described. He contends that in the perversions there is an area of failure of development and integration of the self due to distortions in the primary mother–child relationship; these distortions may be represented either by the excess or by the deficiency of stimulation. Where a depressed mother is unable appropriately to stimulate the child's libidinal potential, the child is compelled to use the surface of the body or its orifices as a substitute, so that erotization comes to hold sway in the growth process.

Perversion may be favoured by the attitude of a mother who idolizes a child that is himself incapable of using objects transitionally. The child very soon begins to understand that the mother perceives him as an idealized part-object and not as a whole person; he learns to practise this dissociation of the experience of self by colluding with the mother for the preservation of the idol-object, which she feels that she herself has created. When the mother finally attempts to distance herself from this exciting and secret complicity, the child is invaded by catastrophic anxieties and threats of annihilation; having failed to construct any real object, he is compelled to reinforce the idolized self still further.

Khan maintains that, with regard to perversion, the seduction theory abandoned by Freud should be reconsidered. The special infantile condition of psychophysical intimacy between mother and child, which is transformed into a process of idolization, traces the outline of the future perverse behaviour. Since idolization corresponds to a form of care that takes no account of real growth, the child will find himself dependent on the first bodily sensations and will attempt to use them to repair the damage done to the development of the self. Because the reparative drive is directed towards the self as an idolized internal object, perversion constitutes a relational experience *sui generis*: the person is never really "another", but instead a transitional object that can be manipulated so as to recreate the omnipotent bond with the mother.

Perversion is by its nature a profoundly solitary technique. Even if two persons are interacting intensely in a "drive-related" manner, it is essentially the invention of a single person: rather than an object relationship, there is a kind of illusory control over the object with the complicity of the other. Control is indispensable: any resistance by the other will break the spell. The whole edifice is designed by the mind; it is only later that the drive functions will be placed in the service of the programmed sexuality.

I shall now summarize three recent contributions on perversion, which, although based on different presuppositions, seem to belong to the theoretical area I have just described—namely, perversion as a defence.

The first is due to Goldberg (1994), a pupil of Kohut, who identifies three fundamental aspects: a specific personal psychodynamic, a split in the sense of reality, and recourse to sexualization. The personal dynamics fuelling the perversion may be numerous, ranging from Oedipal to pre-Oedipal or narcissistic scenarios. Splitting, whose degree varies in accordance with the severity and type of the perversion, is substantially that described by Freud in his paper on fetishism (1927e). Goldberg does not distinguish between perverse manifestations and structured perversions, but merely describes a single type of perversion, which I call episodic or perverse acting out. Incidentally, Goldberg includes occasional homosexuality among the perversions.

Anxiety due to lack of cohesion of the self triggers the sexualized defence. Like other patients with a narcissistic structure, the pervert depends on an external object to maintain the cohesion and vitality of the self; the sexualization is seen as having both a defensive and a relational meaning. Goldberg describes the case of a patient who, during analysis, develops a compulsive homosexuality in which fellatio is stated to represent an attempt at idealized union with a grandiose homosexual self, as reparation of a primal narcissistic wound.

The second contribution is that of Bach (1994), who sees perversion as the outcome of a failed separation from the mother figure. In his view, the denial of separateness involves an incessant search for perverse object relationships; sadism is then a denial of separation and masochism a result of separation anxiety. The sadist is sexually excited by the punishment he inflicts on his object, and thereby develops the omnipotent idea of controlling the object for all time. The masochist, on the other hand, identifies with the lost object, whose loss he disavows by desperately attaching himself to some substitute. The sexual excitation resulting from pain constitutes evidence of the object's permanence for the patient.

For Bach, the crucial factor determining whether the child will tend towards perversion or relational love is the fate of two basic fantasies, the beating fantasy and the fantasy of the maternal phallus.

Although Bach's hypotheses are superficially attractive, they are unconfirmed clinically.

My third author is McDougall (1980, 1993, 1995) who combines the French psychoanalytic tradition with relational sources and inspirations.

McDougall (1993, 1995) regards the so-called perverse sexualities (fetishism, sadomasochistic practices, voyeurism and exhibitionism) simply as extreme and complex attempts to maintain some kind of human relationship; in her opinion, perversion exists only when the individual is completely indifferent to the other's needs and wishes. However, this author rejects the term "perversion" and suggests that it should be replaced by "neo-sexuality", along the lines of the "neo-realities" created by borderline patients in the illusory, if not actually delusional, attempt to find solutions to unresolvable conflicts.

By her proposed new terminology, McDougall seeks to point out that many deviations are tantamount to creations conceived by the psyche down to the very last detail. She sees the masturbatory fantasies of perverts as a metaphorical form of theatrical representation: the heterosexual, homosexual, and autoerotic inventions represent the best possible solution, constructed long ago by the child in response to contradictory parental communications about gender identity, masculinity, or femininity, and his or her assigned sexual role. Since these "neo-sexualities" concern different psychosexual structures, it is appropriate to speak of neo-sexualities in "heterosexuality", in "homosexuality", and in "auto-sexuality". This last category refers to fetishistic or sadomasochistic practices carried on in absolute solitude.

The "neo-sexual solutions" are regarded as attempts by the subject to protect himself from, and treat himself for, a terrifying sense of libidinal death. In addition to the concept of "neo-sexuality", McDougall uses that of "neo-needs", in which the sexual activity or object is constantly sought after as if it were a drug. Addictive dependence as a solution to psychic suffering serves a twofold narcissistic purpose: to repair a damaged self and to preserve the illusion of controlling the object.

McDougall, working with analysands who use sexuality like a drug, stresses the existence of primitive pregenital emotional states infiltrated with sadism and anal erotism.

The third paradigm

Theories derived from Kleinian thought

These theories are based on the Freudian conception of the life and death drives that flowed from the theoretical revision of 1920–1924.

The libidinal drive model having been superseded, the conflict underlying psychopathology is considered to result from the conflictual coexistence of the life drive and the destructive drive, and the outcome of the conflict is seen as determining the subject's form of development and mental growth.

Melanie Klein's theoretical standpoint does not develop in greater depth the biological aspect dear to Freud, but focuses on clinical work. The Kleinian conception, purged of the determinism and fatalism implicit in some aspects of Freud's speculation, confronts the vicissitudes of the destructive drive in the field of primitive development.

Klein (1932) contends that the sadistic components evident in children's fantasies are analogous in some respects to those present in adult criminals. While emphasizing the importance of sadism in the occurrence of mental disturbances, Klein does not follow up this observation of hers by an investigation of perversion, which is also absent from her case histories. However, her theory proves to be important for an understanding of the perversions.

Klein describes the early development of sexuality as a means of facing infantile terrors; this sexualization is liable to give rise to excited states and sexual perversions in adulthood. From the beginning of life the two drives are opposed to each other, and the development of the mind centres on the innate conflict between destructiveness and libido. This conception anticipates the theory of the psychotic and non-psychotic parts of the personality subsequently enunciated by Bion (1957).

The Kleinian and post-Kleinian theories see the perverse patient as split into two non-communicating parts struggling to dominate the personality: the perverse part, interested in domination and sadism, tends to prevail over the healthy part.

Rosenfeld (1988) is mainly concerned with the masochistic submission (passivity) of the infantile part of the self to the destructive narcissistic structures; his are not specific studies of sexual perversion, but contributions on borderline or psychotic structures.

Meltzer (1966, 1973), for his part, offers a theoretical discussion of sexual perversion, which he attributes to incomplete splitting between good and bad sexuality.

Where the fantasy of good sexuality predominates, the parents love each other, and children are born of their union, whereas in bad sexuality the primal scene coincides with the fantasy of a destructive encounter between the parents, in which the children are killed. Some patients in whom splitting and idealization have been insufficient are unable to separate good from bad sexuality.

Meltzer (1973) distinguishes perversion, as an organized aspect of psychic life, from perversity, which may either become organized into perversion or remain as it is.

In "Structural revision of the theory of the perversions and addictions" (Meltzer, 1973), this author likens perversions to drug addictions. In perversion, the dependence on good objects, which is a component of good relationships in both adults and infants, is changed into passivity and submission to bad parts of the self, in a mental state of desperation. "Passivity" must be distinguished from "dependence". To secure the passivity of the good objects, the perverse part falsifies psychic reality by sophisticated seduction techniques. Perversion contains all the elements of the narcissistic organization of drug addiction: the attack on truth, the reduction of the object to a fetishistic plaything, autoerotic sensuality, assumption of the status of victim, and sadistic fantasy. Perversion may become transformed into the perversion of addiction or into criminal perversion.

In "The origins of the fetishistic plaything of sexual perversions" (*ibid.*), Meltzer maintains that the objects of sexual excitation around which perversions crystallize are "dismantled objects", which differ from part-objects. He extends the concept of the fetish by introducing the term "fetishistic plaything". Perverts, like children who have suffered from early autism, dismantle the object by "differentiation" of the senses. Perverse patients do not operate in accordance with the ordinary processes of splitting, but effect the dismantling by selective attention to the sensory qualities of the external object. The formation of the fetish corresponds, in Meltzer's view, to an autoerotic level of sensuality that stands in the way of emotionality, memory and satisfaction.

The hypotheses on sensory dismantling are useful for understanding states of ecstatic sensuality in both autistic and perverse patients.

In *The Claustrum* (1992), Meltzer resumes his consideration of perversion and states that the faecal penis of perversion is a self-object, made up of a disappointing object and of an anti-emotional, cold, primitive part of the self. The excitation therefore does not result from the heat of the drive but contains the coldness of distance and degradation.

In the penultimate chapter of this book, entitled "The claustrum and the perversions/addictions", Meltzer writes that destructiveness forfeits its drive-related connotation in perversion and instead takes on the character of an aversion to the turbulence and passion of the emotions. Hence the characteristic perverse defence against the emotions and the pleasure of life—and not only against mental pain. The essence of the faecal penis of the addictive type of perversion is coldness rather than cruelty. The enemy is the cold, devious serpent and not Milton's Satan, whose envy is mitigated by warmth and admiration.

There may be a progressive transition from habitual perversion to the addictive and finally to the criminal type, by way of a process of ongoing degradation.

Robert Stoller's trauma theory

Robert Stoller cannot easily be assigned to any of the three paradigms described above.

Rather than being a theorist of psychoanalysis, Stoller was a researcher whose investigations centred on sexuality in its multiple forms of expression. Although he was a practising analyst, he does not seem to refer to any psychoanalytic theory and mostly uses descriptive-type parameters for understanding.

Stoller shuns theories because he implicitly feels that they are liable to alter the meaning of the experience under examination. He looks at sexuality, not psychosexuality.

Stoller produced a large number of publications on perversion (e.g. 1975, 1985), drawn not so much from his psychoanalytic experience as from investigations in fields seemingly remote from it, such as the study of human behaviour in conditions of isolation (prisons), or the psychic consequences of severe traumas or of "boundary experiences".

A central aspect of his theory is the notion that perverse erotic excitation is closely bound up with hostility. According to this hypothesis, in perversion the wish to harm another person stems from the need to reverse the infantile situation in which the child was the victim of oppression or a trauma.

A fantasy of revenge translated into action serves to transform the infantile humiliation into adult triumph. Stoller succinctly expressed this concept in his definition of "perversion as the erotic form of hatred": the aversion commonly aroused in us all by perversion reflects the obscure awareness that every perverse act conceals a secret destructive purpose.

In the growing infant, trauma gives rise to a crisis in the development of the person and of gender identity. Perversion, for Stoller, results from a complex family dynamic which, by arousing anxiety or traumatizing the infantile psyche, forces the child to flee from the Oedipal situation that is also one of his aims. Perversion is therefore a disappointed heterosexuality (Stoller, 1975). The perverse act in itself is a reversed reproduction of the old trauma, due to an affective component such as sexualized hate.

While superficially plausible, Stoller's aetiopathogenetic hypotheses are in fact not at all convincing. It is often impossible to identify the trauma, and, even where it exists, a direct connection between it and the perversion cannot be demonstrated. Furthermore, the presence of a feeling such as hate appears inconsistent with perversion, which by its very nature is located in the area of the absence of passion.

As he progresses with his investigation, Stoller seems to attempt fewer and fewer exhaustive formulations to summarize his findings: perversion emerges as a complex entity, still partly indecipherable, in which infantile traumatic experiences, environmental factors and subjective experiences are intertwined.

Stoller's contribution is not amenable to any systematization. His discoveries on the formation of gender identity (1992) remain fundamental. He stresses the existence of a gender identity that predates the discovery of the difference between the sexes. The sense of belonging to one sex or the other arises very early on and remains unchanged throughout life.

In Stoller's view, this unalterable nucleus of gender identity (I am a man/I am a woman) must be distinguished from the more subtle set of convictions (I am male/I am female), whose development is more complicated, which are acquired only after the child has learned what the parents mean by masculinity and femininity. The anatomy of the external genitalia serves as an indication to the parents, who may thus assign the neonate to the relevant sex; later, with the production of sensations, the genitals contribute to the constitution of the primitive bodily ego, the sense of self and the awareness of gender.

An important component—the relationship between the parents and the neonate—is based on parental expectations concerning the neonate's gender identity, the respective gender identity of the parents, the child's identifications with both sexes, libidinal gratification and frustration, and all other aspects of pre-Oedipal and Oedipal development. Stoller asserts that gender identity is determined primarily by post-natal psychological forces, which are independent of the anatomy and physiology of the external genitalia.

On female sexuality, Stoller calls into question Freud's contention that it is diphasic, with a first phase of masculine characteristics preceding the second in which the feminine characteristics proper are acquired. For Freud there is no primary aspect of femininity, attainable only after the resolution of conflicts, the overcoming of disappointment and the renunciation of the penis. Stoller's concept of primary femininity contrasts with Freud's notion of secondary, defensive femininity: Stoller is not putting forward an essentialist, innate view of gender. To establish his gender identity, a boy must disidentify from the mother and identify with the father; his developmental journey is thus more complicated than a girl's. Whereas Freud's position was that masculinity was the natural state and femininity, in favourable cases, was a positive modification of masculinity, Stoller considered that men encountered specific problems in the development of their own masculinity.

Stoller's studies of gender identity are linked to his hypotheses on the genesis of perversion. He is here quite remote from psychoanalytic drive theory, in which castration anxiety is seen as a central element in the aetiology of perversion. The post-Freudian analysts have maintained that perversion is more frequent in men because boys have to face the threat of castration. Since his approach places a different emphasis on genetic aspects and assigns more importance to the influence of the parents than to the strength of the drive, Stoller presents an alternative hypothesis: in his view, because it is more difficult for boys than for girls to emerge from symbiosis with the mother and arrive at a male identity, they are more likely, in the course of this complex journey, to undergo traumas or environmental pressures that might interfere with their psychosexual development and facilitate their entry into perversion.

Stoller's important innovation is to see gender identity not as an individual fact depending on anatomy, the quality of the drive and its potential active or passive availability, but as determined by the expectations, or, better, the imagination, of the parents and the psychological pressure they exert on the neonate. In other words, regardless of the child's anatomical sex, the parents can influence the very basis of his or her sexual psychic identity, which then remains a constant. In Stoller's view, then, there is a conflict between nature and culture, in which culture prevails.

Whereas for Freud the outcome of the process of developing a full male or female role identity is uncertain because it depends on the vicissitudes of a large number of identifications (with the father, the mother, the active or passive, sadistic or masochistic position) within Oedipal triangulation, Stoller seems to disregard Freud's lesson and takes no account of the part played by the imagination and by sexual fantasy in the choice of sexual identity. On the contrary, he attributes the child's sexual choice to the environment, and primarily to the wishes of the child's care-givers. The assignment of identity takes precedence over the evidence of anatomy; the problem is of inter-generational transmission rather than the effect of the sexual drive. The importance assigned by Stoller to primal components and environmental pressure partly removes sexual identity problems from the sphere of Freud's masculinity/femininity dichotomy and activity/passivity polarity, and detaches them once and for all from that of sexual perversion.

Some reflections on the biological aspect

With the introduction of psychic and motivational parameters, drive theory sees sexuality as the engine of the production of pleasure and offers an interpretation of both normal and pathological development.

However, "libido" or "libidinal drives" cannot be invoked to facilitate understanding of a phenomenon as complex as sexual pleasure (Stoller, 1992).

Even today, human sexuality appears as a territory yet to be explored; our knowledge of its intimate nature, as well as of the interaction between psychological and biological components, is still limited.

The drive, as the psychic representative of biological stimuli and processes within the body, is a boundary concept between the somatic and the psychic. Having located perversion within the framework of human psychosexual development, Freud concentrated on the particular nature of sexuality. However, the mystery is only seemingly resolved. Although adduced for the purpose of explanation in psychoanalytic theory, sexuality itself still remains to be explained (Imbasciati, 1997).

The sadomasochistic perversion, which flies in the face of the ordinary rules for obtaining pleasure, compounds the enigma of human sexuality even further.

Although he regarded sexuality as the key to the interpretation of psychic life, Freud always had in mind the biological mystery of the pleasure of sexuality: he wrote more than once that scientific investigation would sooner or later identify the biochemical substances underlying the mechanisms of sexual excitation and orgasm. Even today, despite the discovery of a large number of substances involved in sexual development and libido, the biochemistry of sexual pleasure remains unknown.

Sexual pleasure stems from a special psychic state obtained by manipulation of the body and involving a withdrawal from the rest of the world; yet this state cannot be attributed solely to the effect of perceptual afferences, of however many different kinds, since the psychic function is not confined to the integration of bodily and visceral perceptions.

Oddly enough, human anatomy and physiology show that the genital organs lack a specific receptor for sexual pleasure. The absence of specialized organs suggests that sexual orgasm is determined by a bodily process with an additional psychic component, which makes use of sensations of a number of different kinds—tactile, visceral, visual and olfactory—and which ultimately becomes a purely psychic fact. For this reason, erotic pleasure cannot be seen as a single-component experience; we should instead think in terms of multiple excitations differing from one individual to another, and—what is even more complicated—of excitations that differ within one and the same person.

Depending on the type of construction created by experience and personal history, particular subjective imaginative constellations pave the way for orgasm. All perceptions are additively channelled by the imagination towards the discharge of pleasure on the basis of a mentally constructed experience.

Owing to its imaginative component, erotic excitation is highly sophisticated, so that man is the only living organism whose sexual bond represents a continuum. The traces of infantile sensual experience, symbolic association and, in particular, the aesthetic value of the object have the function of sustaining desire.

The sexual experience arises out of a complex interplay of fantasy and experience. Yet there is something mechanical and almost standardized in the regulation of sexual excitation. Since each individual has a personal sexual stereotype bound up with a given constellation of stimuli, sexual excitation becomes a kind of chain reaction, programmable through a set of sensory or aesthetic components capable of triggering specific fantasies. Within the couple, a summation and strengthening of excitation takes place, and the excitation of one partner becomes the vehicle for the involvement of the other.[1]

The state of excitation always to some extent involves the presence of a fetish: the more the love object is created in the imagination, the more the excitation is aroused through the fetish, which is the vehicle of omnipotent fantasies—hence its constant presence in perversion.

Even if the split between sex and love does not constitute a sufficient definition of perversion, it is nevertheless a prerequisite for the enjoyment of sexual pleasure. An encounter of this kind precludes any relationship involving help or psychological understanding between the partners.

Perversion is enigmatic because, apart from the absence of love, pleasure is obtained through sensations that are normally experienced as unpleasurable: it is a special pleasure obtained by a paradoxical method.

Freud several times stresses the primacy of pleasure:

> [...] we have every reason to believe that sensations of pain, like other unpleasurable sensations, trench upon sexual excitation and produce a pleasurable condition, for the sake of which the subject will even willingly experience the unpleasure of pain. [Freud, 1915c, p. 128]

or

> [...] while [...] pains are being inflicted on other people, they are enjoyed masochistically by the subject through his identification of himself with the suffering object. In both cases, of course, it is not the pain itself which is enjoyed, but the accompanying sexual excitation. [*ibid.*, p. 129]

The enigma seems to lie in the element of pleasure—the "accompanying sexual excitation".

For this reason, limiting the investigation to the field of sexuality alone does not do justice to the complexity of perversion. It is necessary to take account of other facts, observed outside the sexual context, that forge unusual links between psychic experience and the data of biology, whereby the complex dynamics of pleasure can be further investigated.

It has been demonstrated that, outside the field of perversion proper, traumas or boundary experiences of suffering can be transformed into intensely pleasurable sensations.

At the 1998 Fall Meeting of the American Psychoanalytic Association, Stoller showed how the subject's state of consciousness is altered during sadomasochistic practices. This alteration is similar to the ecstasy of certain religious experiences (those of flagellants) and the dissociated state described by political prisoners who have survived torture. Some patients who have had a near-death experience resulting from severe trauma or major surgery can later re-create the anxiety-inducing sensation of death or dying and transform it into voluptuous suffering.

Future biochemical research on sensual pleasure will surely bring us closer to understanding the mysterious link between pleasure and pain, and may reveal the sensory parameters involved at body level in the sadomasochistic perversion.

For the moment, we may suppose that pain-derived orgasmic pleasure is due to the endorphins, which are produced by the body itself as a protection from pain and which bind to the same receptors as drugs. A classical example is the excitation, or "buzz", experienced by athletes training for track events in their constant attempts to break records. They report the development of a sensation of euphoria in their regular training over longer and longer distances. It may be postulated that running gives rise to a state of stress whereby endogenous opioids that act on the brain's pleasure system are released (R. F. Thompson, 1993).

If endorphins are mobilized in painful states and in sexual experience, it is not unreasonable to suppose that, through pain, the masochist seeks (and obtains) the triggering of endorphin-mediated pleasure.

Note

1. The most common technique for programming excitation is pornography. The reader is carried along by the vision of other people's intercourse through identification with one partner or the other or with both.

CHAPTER NINE

After the theories

"Is man master of his penchants? One must feel sorry for those who have strange tastes, but never insult them. Their wrong is Nature's too; they are no more responsible for having come into the world with tendencies unlike ours than are we for being born bandy-legged or well-proportioned"

de Sade, 1795, p. 188

"But, it may well be asked, can a person be so completely false to his own nature? even for one moment? If the answer is no, then there is no way to explain the mysterious mental process by which we crave things we actually do not want at all, is there?"

Mishima, 1960, p. 81

A valid theoretical hypothesis cannot close itself off and disregard a part of the phenomena it sets out to explain, but must be open to all the constellations present. If any element cannot be integrated into the construction, that construction will thereby be weakened.

What unites the three theoretical paradigms identified in the previous chapter and what divides them? What remains unexplored? What distortions and ambiguities in clinical and therapeutic practice are observable?

What is sexuality? What does sexual pleasure consist in? Is there really such a thing as a normal sexuality? What are the means for achieving excitation and orgasm? If infantile sexuality exists, how does it differ from its adult counterpart? Does an element of aggression form part of a normal love relationship? Is aggression different from destruction? Does perverse sexuality form a continuum with the rest of sexual experience?

Having defined the clinical field and described the structural characteristics of sadomasochism, we can compare the various theories and determine how far each takes account of this particular perversion.

I shall examine the underlying fantasy of the perversion, the role of imagination and the process of sexualization, with a view to arriving at a better comparison between the various theoretical approaches. I shall then attempt to examine the meaning assigned by the various theories to the component parts of the perversion, commencing with sexuality and aggression, the mixture of which lies at the root of sadomasochism. Having described the main characteristics, I shall be in a position to present my own view of the sadomasochistic perversion and the corresponding psychoanalytic theories.

Infantile sadomasochistic fantasy

There is an extraordinary continuity between the first infantile "games" and the coming into being of the adult perversion. In analyses of perverse patients the underlying fantasy that led to the perversion can be reconstructed; this complex fantasy will not be limited to the cruel behaviour but will refer back, via the sexual imagination, to the specific object relationship of the perversion. By way of example, I shall describe the basic fantasy underlying the perversion of a 20-year-old male sadomasochistic patient.

In the normal course of events, a boy sits astride a cushion, which, in his fantasy, comes alive and becomes a horse: the boy now possesses a powerful, friendly animal that carries him around, obedient to his commands. The boy derives pleasure from the feeling of power in being the master of a strong animal that wants to serve the rider in every way it can.

Let us now consider the version of this game described by the patient.

We still have a boy playing at riding a horse, but this time he is concerned primarily with the animal and its sensations: the horse must gallop faster and faster, carrying the rider on as quickly as it can; it must positively fly. In this version of the game, what is important is not so much the exciting sense of rapid motion as the pleasure derived from the horse's efforts to give its master the maximum possible satisfaction and pleasure. The pleasure stems from flying higher and higher (the boy presses his body into the cushion, squashes the horse, sinks his spurs into its sides) but, in particular, from his mount's devoted suffering as it does its utmost for the rider. The boy reaches the acme of pleasure when the horse has given its all to comply with his commands; and the sight of the exhausted animal turns the excitation into sensual pleasure.

The boy's infantile imagination generates the figure of the animal-as-slave, whose "altruistic" services give rise to sexual excitation. Intent on serving the other's pleasure, the object sacrifices itself, and it is its very self-immolation that excites pleasure. The object's enslavement is not obtained by violence, as the horse spontaneously wishes to sacrifice itself for the sake of the rider's triumph.

In the dyadic unity of master and slave, the two protagonists have different and complementary roles that serve a single excitatory purpose. The master takes pleasure in drawing energy from the slave, while the latter's supreme good is to sacrifice himself to his master's pleasure.

What implications does this have for our two boys and their sexuality?

We may suppose that, in the first boy, the infantile game—the pleasure of mastery or control—will encourage the development of the sense of autonomy and of skills, thus helping to structure the personality. In the second child, the excitation of power, having entered the realm of sexuality, constructs a world of imaginary relationships within the master–slave dyad. The fantasy built up on these foundations persists during childhood and adolescence and ultimately becomes the only way of achieving orgasm.

In the case of perversion, the sadomasochistic scene, while always remaining identical to itself, assumes an infinite number of variant forms. Pleasure may be derived from illustrations in books (the slave, the wounded boxer, or the bleeding body of Christ); or horror tales may be the stimulus for the construction of stories that increase sexual excitation; or parts of the body may stage sequences from a sadomasochistic drama (the masturbating hand represents a sadistic man and the tortured penis becomes an abused little boy). Through the power of the imagination, the subject and the characters created are all one.

In a later version of the infantile sadomasochistic fantasy, the position of the dominator gives way to that of the dominated. The dominator, remaining within the dual unity, can enjoy masochistic and sadistic pleasure simultaneously. The same child who thrills to the horse game may become an adolescent who puts on black boots and dreams of being a Nazi officer abusing a little boy. In his imagination, he may at one and the same time be the officer and the boy, so as to enjoy the pleasure of both.

The description of the infantile sadomasochistic fantasy illustrates Freud's particular contribution to the role of infantile sexuality in the development of perversion. Stressing that the roots of the sadomasochistic perversion lie in infancy, Freud demonstrated the early onset of sexual pleasure and fantasies. The sadomasochistic fantasy stems from infantile omnipotence, which constructs a world in the service of the subject and dedicated to the subject's pleasure. In perversion, however, the infantile world loses the free creativity of play and becomes dependent on the exciting power of the sexual imagination, which remains locked into the single scheme of dominator–dominated.

The early fixation of infantile sexuality on the masturbatory imagination explains the absence of relational sexuality in the adult pervert, for whom sadomasochistic sexual pleasure is superior to any love relationship. The creation of a satisfying world of fantasy leads to psychic withdrawal.

The role of the imagination in perversion

It is the imagination that accounts for the central role of the visual function in the construction of the perverse scene and for the importance of the aesthetic–voyeuristic component of the resulting pleasure. Looking as a way of capturing and incorporating the other; being looked at or wounding the other's look in exhibitionism; and the excited concentration on the sexual organs in pornography —all these form part of the imaginary scenery indispensable to perversion.

I use the term "imagination" in the sense of a waking fantasy, as understood by Freud and as described by Anna Freud in her paper "The relation of beating-phantasies to a day-dream" (1923), although with the more specific connotation of a world of one's own called into being by the imagination.[1]

Objects live only to the extent that they perform the task assigned to them by the imagination; a sexual encounter is a repetition of what has been pre-thought and imagined, involving little spontaneity and no freedom. These aspects are responsible for what an external observer sees as the dehumanized, repetitive nature of perverse acts.

The pervert generates his own omnipotent fantasy through the relationship with the partner created in imagination: to achieve pleasure, he must create a new reality. If the partner were experienced as alive and independent, the freedom and omnipotence of fantasy could not exist; a real partner with his or her own requirements and needs sets a limit to the imagination and, as such, diminishes the level of excitation.

The pervert is a producer who cannot countenance the existence of a co-producer and who, in the choreography of fantasy, may believe himself to be the emperor who can dispose totally of the slave—a slave utterly devoted to the satisfaction of his wishes.

Sacher-Masoch (1875, p. 50) writes: "With me everything has its roots in the imagination, and thence it receives its nourishment". Havelock Ellis (1913) was the first to draw attention to the role of imagination. He was convinced that the main source of pleasure lay in imagining and that an important component was the possibility of exchanging and reversing roles by means of a "vivid imagination".

In Ryu Murakami's film *Tokyo Decadence*, at the end of a prolonged mistress–slave sadomasochistic sequence, the two protagonists take off their "costumes" and exchange contrite and well-mannered greetings as they arrange their next meeting. The unexpected transformation of the two partners into a courteous, well-bred lady and gentleman gives rise to a sudden derealizing and humorously liberating effect in the audience. In my view, this sequence is an exemplary illustration of the alienating effect of the split in the pervert's psychic life—a split between the life of the imagination, in which it is possible to roam freely in excitation, and the return to real life.

However, the imaginative act of perversion goes beyond the dimension of representation on a stage, where it is pleasurable to direct the drama from a position half-way between fiction and reality—moving in and out as in the above example.

A better characterization of the role of imagination in the achievement of pleasure in perversion can be found in Maria Marcus's autobiography *A Taste for Pain* (1981), which is cited in Bill Thompson's *Sadomasochism* (1994). Marcus tells us that, during her schooldays, her mind was continually excited by accounts of tribal initiation rites, scenes of violence in barracks, episodes of slavery, Chinese tortures, atrocities practised by the Ancient Romans, etc.; these aroused powerful emotions in her, but not sexual experiences proper. When her overflowing imagination produced real scenes of torture and punishment, the young girl realized that she could use reality only if it were remote enough not to appear as such, but instead as fantasy. At this point she could subjugate it and use it as a "thing", a sexual stimulus. As an adult, she came to be attracted by rough and violent men, encounters with whom were more pleasurable the more brutal they were. However, if a certain threshold was exceeded and the encounters became too painful or dangerous, fear and suffering inhibited the pleasure.

She then discovered that the experience that had frightened her could be used later to construct fantasies leading to pleasure. Finally, having understood the importance of the psychic aspect, she would indulge in numerous symbolic acts of humiliation, of shame and of being a person of no consequence. She discovered that being an "instrument" or "object" of the "master" gave pleasure only if it was she who controlled her own "submission". She understood that it was only her active control of these symbolic acts that aroused her; only the reality constructed in her imagination was necessary to set her on the path of pleasure. Reality was usable only if wholly created by her mind.

The sadomasochistic monad and the unity of opposites

In ordinary sexual intercourse the couple have the perception of a mutual pleasure; the involvement of one partner helps to raise the other's level of pleasure and, if all goes well, the result is the state of loss of boundaries and bodily fusion that coincides with orgasm. The relationship is one of equality, and the pleasure, which is both shared and specular, lies in yielding to the other's pleasure without demanding the appropriation of all the pleasure to oneself.

In sadomasochism, by contrast, only one protagonist must experience all the pleasure; the more his partner has no pleasure or experiences unpleasure, the more satisfied he is. The asymmetry of the relationship emphasizes the value of hierarchic power: the sadist is aroused by domination and the masochist by the active pleasure of submission.

The roles must be kept rigidly complementary: the pleasure stems from the perception of one's own sensations coupled with that derived from the unequal position of the other. The fusion achieved between the partners has particular characteristics; the integration of bodies and mutual sensations follows more complex pathways.

The sadist achieves orgasm when the masochistic object becomes yielding and dominable. Conversely, the masochist's excitation is proportional to the degree of active fusion with the sadist's pleasure; orgasm depends not on mere passivity but on self-annihilation and identification with the sadist, such that the masochist makes the sadist's pleasure his own.

The perverse orgasm thus entails a total identification: only the complete submission of the masochistic partner to his sadistic counterpart, which creates a mixture of two contrasting entities, leads to pleasure. The fusion of bodies also takes place in normal sexual relations, and its achievement, with the consequent loss of boundaries and the feeling of total mutual interpenetration, leads to orgasm. The excitation of perversion, however, results not so much from the fusion of the two bodies, both dominated by the same desire, as from the fascination of complementary roles and representations: on top/underneath, dominator/dominated, active/ passive, master/slave, etc.

The important elements are the complementarity and exchange

brought about by the interpenetration of roles at the very moment of the sexual encounter. The pervert wants to be both the masturbating, torturing hand and the masturbated, tortured penis. The enslavement witnessed and enjoyed by both sides thus brings about the unity of opposites, whereby all the available pleasure can be appropriated to oneself. As Sacher-Masoch wrote, to achieve ecstatic sensual pleasure one has to be both anvil and hammer. The pervert must incorporate his own sensations as the dominator and at the same time, identifying with the other, enjoy the pleasure of being dominated.

I introduce the concept of the "sadomasochistic monad" to describe the fusional and masturbatory combined figure that appropriates the pleasure of both partners. The sadomasochistic monad has the subject's own body as its locus and has no need of the other: in the mirror, the pervert can visualize the sadomasochistic scene on himself and put aggressor and victim together. During masturbation the pleasure of both the beater and the beaten is fantasized: in this scene, the pervert tortures the penis, beats his own testicles and sees penile erection as a token of the excitation of the person being beaten.

Bergler (1938) reports on the case of a patient who had the fantasy of torturing a woman, stabbing her breasts and forcing objects into her anus. In enacting such tortures on himself, the patient fantasized another person acting as the aggressor.

Sexualization in perversion

Psychoanalytic theory has a large number of complex constructions to explain the meaning of sexuality, and in particular its non-relational forms.

It is essential to distinguish between what is primitive and capable of developing, on the one hand, and what constitutes a psychopathological structure, on the other.

Freud's reference (1919e) to children who very early on—at the age of four or five—develop a fantasy capable of inducing sexual pleasure tells us that sexual orgasm may be a mental fact earlier in time than the real action of masturbation.

To understand the nature of perversion, it is very important to use the term sexualization rather than sexuality. This distinction involves the notion of different categories of sexual experience with mental states differing from that of ordinary sexuality, which is inconsistent with Freud's unitary model of sexual energy. In his account of the case of Senatspräsident Schreber, who dreamed that he could experience female orgasm, Freud comes close to understanding such conditions, but fails to classify them appropriately.[2]

States of perverse sexualization seem to be very widespread in severe mental pathologies; Alvarez (1992), for example, refers to them in her accounts of the therapy of autistic children.

The self-excitatory experience seems to have particular characteristics in some perverts. The fetishistic patient described by Joseph (1971), who dressed from head to foot in a rubber garment, could ejaculate only through stimulation of the skin.

Like erotic dreams that cause the dreamer to ejaculate, sexualized fantasies can cause orgasm. Subjects who exhibit perverse behaviour may have particular sexual excitability. Because the imagination is so powerful, sexual orgasm can be achieved without the intermediary of the body; in such cases the mind behaves like a continuous generator of sexual excitation.[3]

Hartmann (1964) refers to the sexualization of the ego functions, which he regards as a sign of regressive displacement close to psychic disintegration. For this reason he introduces the concept of neutralization or desexualization, which must not be confused with that of drive sublimation. Neutralization means that the sexual fantasy, instead of being repressed, is deprived of its sexual or aggressive clothing by a transformation of energy.

Kohut (quoted in Goldberg, 1994) constructed a similar model of neutralization in maintaining that archaic fantasies are transposed into tractable and non-sexual parts of the psyche. This transposition is deemed an integral part of analytic treatment, like the progressive diminution of repression.

Coen (1981) suggests that the term "sexualization" should be used only for a sexual fantasy or behaviour having a clearly defensive purpose.

If we are to understand the world of perverse sexualization, we must in my view set aside the parameter of psychosexuality.

Some authors, including several classifiable within the second paradigm (see Chapter 8)—e.g. Glover (1933, 1964); Gillespie (1956);

Khan (1979); Stolorow (1979) and Goldberg (1994)—have used this term and attempted to clarify it, but areas of ambiguity persist.

If energy-based concepts are abandoned, a form of sexualization that can be clearly distinguished from the usual modes of sexual activity can indeed be described. Goldberg, in particular, considers that sexuality, coupled with splitting, is one of the distinctive features of perversion. In his view, sexualization is not a defence but an attempt to make up a structural deficit. Basically, perverse sexual fantasies and behaviour that give rise to pleasure in domination or sexual pleasure proper have the defensive function of preventing further regression.

Goldberg differentiates sexualization from sexuality because he would not otherwise be able to distinguish between certain pathological forms of homosexual activity that can be modified and others which are unmodifiable. His thesis is that normal sexual activity calls for a stable, cohesive self. Conversely, sexualization, which serves to maintain the self temporarily, comes to the fore only when one or other of the self-objects are in danger.

Whereas Goldberg thus on the one hand denies that sexualization is a defence, on the other he believes that it is used to make up structural deficits in the self. The concept of defence is admittedly not easy to define, but nevertheless I hold that the function of making up structural defects may constitute a defensive operation. While emphasizing the importance of sexualization, Goldberg fails to distinguish between sexualization as a defence against anxiety and as an element of a pathological structure.

In my view, it is not the weak self that turns to sexualization in order to find integration, but rather sexualization that weakens the self and contributes to evacuating it. In fact, I see sexualization as a component of a psychopathological structure, and not as a defensive operation to ward off anxiety, pain or collapse of the self. In the case of overwhelming anxieties such as those of borderline patients, sexual excitation may be involved in their control and may lead to a perverse state of pleasure that has nothing to do with perversion proper.

Like Goldberg, other authors with the same theoretical leanings have difficulty in conceptualizing sexualization because, despite having abandoned the straitjacket of the theory of psychosexual development, they do not accept the hypothesis of a psychopathological organization centred on masturbatory sexuality functioning as an addictive space or retreat. For them, "sexuality" is always relational, operating in support of the self as a counter to anxiety.

In *The Problem of Perversion*, Goldberg (1994) illustrates his concept of sexual perversion with some case histories which, in my view, are merely examples of anomalous sexual behaviour. Discussing a doctor patient of his who would, on impulse, force his female patients to fellate him, he writes that this behaviour could be defined as perversion because it was episodic, associated with anxiety and followed by what the patient called a sense of guilt, which, however, was often clearly shame.

Goldberg disregards the fact that the pathological structure present in perversion can eliminate anxiety, guilt and shame because it colonizes and subdues the conscious parts of the self, unlike impulsive forms of sexual behaviour, which entail conflict and hence guilt, anxiety and shame.

Sexualization can be described more easily on the basis of a Kleinian model. Considering the origins of the concept whereby sexual experience is distinguished according to whether it is used defensively or relationally, we find that Klein (1932) was the first to note that sexuality, where its onset is precocious, must be seen as a means of confronting primitive anxieties.

Yet sexualization is not a mere defence mechanism. If it were, it would be impossible to explain how it could ever progressively and stably become an anti-relational and anti-emotional psychopathological structure that monopolizes and dominates the psychic world.

An excellent description of this process is given by Meltzer (1966), in his discussion of the mechanisms of anal masturbation. The model he proposes is that of a child who tries to avoid the anxiety of separation from the mother by turning to his own buttocks, which he idealizes as the absent breast; the excitation of anal masturbation abolishes the perception of loss and replaces it with a sexual short circuit. Meltzer (1973) calls these particular conditions "sexual states of mind".

Sexualization is a withdrawal of the mind into a private world based on the sexualized distortion of perceptions that underlies all forms of perversion. Paedophiles, in particular, may feel that the world is a set of sexualized relations, that the children they desire are in turn full of sexual desires, and that it is impossible to forgo this unique source of pleasure.

The sexualized state is unconsciously symbolized as a feared condition capable of capturing the self and of giving rise to an irreversible mental and emotional deficiency (De Masi, 1988; Meltzer, 1973).

A perverse male patient dreamed that a little boy was abducted and taken to Oriental brothels in order to be abused. On his return, the child's appearance had changed: he had the face of a "mongol", an idiot. A female patient trying to emerge from a sexualized state dreamed that, while house-hunting with her daughter, she was offered accommodation in a confined space in which she could stand up only if engaged in sexual intercourse with a man. She decided not to go inside because she knew that if she did she would lose her daughter.

Dreams illustrate the deadly nature of the sexualized excitation that keeps such patients going—an awareness that remains unconscious unless worked through in the analytic relationship. The pathological organization offers perverse gratifications so exciting that they prove to be irresistible for a long time.

The concept of sexualization takes perversion out of the Freudian system, in which, as we have seen, it is regarded as a stoppage of development at early stages of sexuality—at the polymorphism of infantile sexuality in which situations of domination and aggression predominate.

I myself regard perversion in general, and the sadomasochistic perversion in particular, not as the pathological accentuation of certain infantile component drives, but as a distorted development not only of sexuality but of the entire organization of the personality and mental structure. Sexualization is equivalent to a special, masturbatory kind of mental state, an early withdrawal from reality and from relating to the world. Perversion is not a development of infantile polymorphous sexuality, but a flight and withdrawal that begins in infancy through the production of sexualized mental states.

My own perverse analysands had been deprived, isolated or overstimulated children, who had taken refuge in a sexualized world of fantasy, attracted by the masturbatory mental sensual pleasure constantly produced by their fantasy. I recall one male patient who was accustomed, from a very early age, to spend hours and hours immersed in exciting fantasies. The most frequent concerned a young slave who was so devoted that he would plunge into a well at his command, diving deeper and deeper until he risked suffocation. When the slave's efforts were at their peak, orgasm would be triggered.

Whereas I believe this sexualized withdrawal to be the nucleus and genesis of perversion—indeed, of all perversions—I consider that the sadomasochistic perversion is one of its possible outcomes.

Albeit with due regard to Freud's discovery of infantile sexuality, I emphasize the aspect of the early onset and omnipresence of sexualization, which captures the mind of a delicate child inclined to take flight from the world of human relations.

Sexualization takes the form of a withdrawal that stands in the way of psycho-emotional development and therefore constitutes one of the components of regression, theorized by Freud as fixations to early stages of psychosexuality.

The perverse fantasy becomes established in infancy and gives rise to a closed world that prevents any development towards other types of love relationship; it is a destructive defence that does constant damage to the psyche, which remains trapped in the search for a drugged pleasure.

The fact that the sexualized perverse fantasy is above all a psychic withdrawal also explains why perverse analysands do not erotize or sexualize the transference, as borderline patients are observed to do.

The nature of sadomasochistic pleasure

The distinction between sexuality and sexualization will facilitate understanding of another important component of the sadomasochistic perversion, which also accounts for the special character assumed by pleasure. Freud referred to this aspect in terms of the idealization of the drive.

To define the type of orgasm achieved by a masochist, in his famous novel *Venus in Furs* Sacher-Masoch uses the word *übersinnlich*. This German word means either over-sensory or over-sensual (the Italian translator appropriately understands it in the latter sense[4]), and, in all its senses and shades of meaning, describes a particular sensual pleasure that extends beyond the bounds of ordinary perception and sensibility.

In his famous paper "The masochistic contract", Smirnoff (1969) attributes this sensual pleasure to the iconography of martyrdom, thus identifying a component common to perversion and mystical ecstasy. Perversion is in his view *übersinnlich* precisely because of its ability to capture the mind and provide it with over-sensual (or over-sensitive) experiences—amounting to an ecstatic pleasure resembling the trance state.

The central element of perversion, in Smirnoff's view, lies in the progressive submission to an over-sensual orgasmic pleasure that acts like a hypnotic force. Attention was already drawn to the intensity of the perverse orgasm by Freud (1930a [1929]), who sees it as the satisfaction of an uncontrollable drive. Perhaps, as Chasseguet-Smirgel (1992) points out, hubris—the intoxication of having overthrown the parental procreative universe—plays a part in this kind of excitation. Narcissistic megalomania and hatred of reality are indeed essential to the perverse act.

All this suggests that sexual perversions belong to a mental area akin to that of addiction, for they express a dependence on, or enslavement to, a mental drug of the sexual type, similar to alcohol or narcotic dependence.

Heinz Kohut is perhaps the only analyst to have emphasized the resemblance between perverse pleasure and that derived from taking drugs. He states in his first lecture to the Chicago Institute (Kohut, 1996) that a person is driven to perversion with the same intensity as a drug addict and experiences the same kind of pleasure.

In other words, perversions are techniques for producing a state of mental excitation that is sought for its own sake and does not include any relational element.

An addictive dependence of this kind is more obvious in the extreme cases in which the perversion gradually becomes detached from the sexual encounter proper and becomes a technique for the direct production of the drugged state of mind. This is exemplified by suffocation manoeuvres that give rise to a state of orgasmic mental pleasure—as dramatically illustrated in Nagisa Oshima's famous Japanese film *Empire of the Senses*, whose protagonist, ever more caught up in the search for pleasure, meets his end asphyxiated by his lover after an exhausting immersion in sensual ecstasy.

Cruelty in sadomasochism

As already noted by Freud, children who derive pleasure from sadistic or masochistic fantasies are generally meek, impressionable and averse to manifest cruelty. Adult perverts, too, may appear gentle and sometimes altruistic, involved in the defence of justice and of the weak or persecuted. A person who achieves sexual excitation with sadistic and masochistic fantasies may secretly idealize violence but fear the real aggression of the outside world.

It has been pointed out (Smirnoff, 1969) that the masochist, although presenting himself as the passive partner in the couple, in fact performs an active role. This is because masochistic pleasure stems not only from physical and moral suffering but also from the structure of the play, observance of the casting, and mutual power. The control the masochist knows he has over the sadistic torturer corresponds to the specular role assumed autonomously and willingly by the latter. In the sadomasochistic experience, the sadistic partner must comply with the masochist's requests, just as the masochist must in regard to what binds him to the sadist. For this reason, a contract specifying the functions of each must be concluded. The existence of the contract not only guarantees that certain limits will not be exceeded but also stipulates absolute conformity with the mutually assigned roles.

Michel de M'Uzan (1973) presents the confidences of a masochistic pervert with very severe pathology, obtained in two long interviews during a period of remission. At the time the subject had monstrous mutilations, resulting from his masochistic practices, visible on his chest and back and, specifically, on his genitals and around the anal orifice. Since he achieved pleasure at the acme of suffering, he was compelled to increase the level of pain constantly, and, with it, the level of abuse by the sadistic partner, who often took fright and withdrew. The threshold of pain had to be overcome every time in order to obtain the desired pleasure—an ecstasy in every segment of the body. However, this was not the main thing: what this person wanted was "an abasement of the personality", and what he sought more than anything else was his own "veritable moral suicide". For example, although he did not derive physical satisfaction from being buggered, he would tell his partner that he was homosexual so as to degrade himself morally. Declaring himself to be homosexual was equivalent to an insult coinciding with the need to feel his own will annihilated.

Even if pain is one aspect of the complex interaction of sensations that brings the sadomasochist to orgasm, its experience can be regarded as only one of the tactical conditions involved in the accomplishment of the complex masochistic strategy, whose ultimate purpose is to derive mental pleasure from the subject's own annihilation. In these circumstances, fantasies and actions, however cruel, are not perceived as such, because the cognition of pain and cruelty presupposes maintenance of the perception of the human relationship, which is lacking in this case.

Perversion could be seen as a *folie à deux* centring on a delusional veneration of power and of the violence with which is it exercised— an aberration that needs a complementary, symmetrical partner.

In the sadomasochistic monad, the perception of the difference between victim and aggressor is lost; the cruelty of the action is precluded by the fact of mutual consent and by the fusion of bodies. The excitation leading to pleasure stems from the triumph of perceiving the accomplishment of the object's enslavement; pain, for its part, appears as an inevitable element in the elimination of the vitality and independence of the object, in the object's elimination, or in the partners' mutual elimination and enslavement.

Hence the cruelty implicit in the sadomasochistic act seems not to be the primary object of the perversion. Enduring suffering is an act of dedication and a proof of submission which the master demands in the course of the performance and which the servant longs to offer. To give the maximum of pleasure, the submission must be active and consensual, and not obtained by force.

The sadomasochistic perversion is not usually presented as a narcissistic pathology, but it is easy to show that the driving force behind pleasure in this dimension is precisely narcissism in one of its purest and most extreme forms. I am referring here to narcissism not as an experience of confirmation or idealization of the self, as it is seen in certain psychoanalytic theories, but rather as pleasure in the control and subordination of the other, in the absolute triumph of the self.

Since there is no such thing as pure narcissism, sadomasochism too always involves a dual polarity. The perverse type of narcissistic relationship demands that the subject's own pleasure shall also be the other's. This statement, which at first sight appears paradoxical because it corresponds to the situation in a normal sexual relationship, is characterized in perversion by the principle of asymmetry and falls within the narcissistic polarity of triumph/humiliation.

Pleasure is reserved for one partner only; the other must suffer or be enslaved. The object therefore exists only as a function of the subject's own wish for domination, power and narcissistic triumph. Pleasure is a function of power.

Notes

1. I here distinguish between, on the one hand, imagination as fantasy produced *ex novo* and, on the other, the personal imagination as an act that creates an idealized personal world of memories, thoughts and private wishes. Winnicott uses the term "transitional space" for a mental area that contains the potential for personal development—an individual, private area having a narcissistic-ideal character.
2. Freud describes a similar process in the Wolf Man, in the form of a fusional fantasy in which the patient tries to enter his mother's genitals. The patient identifies with the penis and seeks to achieve orgasm by thrusting himself into the maternal womb.
3. Krafft-Ebing was the first to draw attention to the perverse predisposition of people who exhibit hyperexcitability and a tendency to "sexual ecstasy". The term "sexualization" should not be used in the sense of hypersexuality. Sexualization is a mental state that often accompanies impotence.
4. *Übersinnlich* is borrowed from the words of Mephistopheles to Faust: "Du übersinnlicher, sinnlicher Freier . . ." ["Thou over-sensual, sensual suitor"]. In Italian editions of *Faust*, the word is often translated as "transcendental". As Deleuze (1967) points out, in Goethe's text it means not "over-sensory" but "over-sensual" or "over-carnal", in accordance with the theological tradition in which *Sinnlichkeit* denotes the flesh, *sensualitas*.

CHAPTER TEN

Areas of contiguity

Borderline structures and perverse defences

I should like here to develop some ideas which I have already touched upon in connection with the distinction between perverse–compulsive sexuality and structured perversions.

It is well known that fear and terror, the legacy of infantile impotence, can be used as a source of excitation.

A characteristic feature of many borderline patients is the curious mixture of anxiety, terror and sexual excitation they deploy in order to confront the sense of persecution and the fear of annihilation. In borderline pathology—the borderline being that between the neuroses and the psychoses—the patient has never succeeded in overcoming the persecutory and annihilation anxieties of earliest infancy; he has not had the help of an object capable of assisting him in this task. In these patients, terrifying fantasies, together with the reading of certain kinds of books or the viewing of horror films, often serve as a means of tackling persecutory anxieties or constitute an attempt to overcome or treat them. The anxiety sequences are traversed and contained in excitatory fashion, and as such afford pleasure. The pleasure obtained may be perverse in nature, since it entails a degree of cruel excitation, but does not amount to an actual perversion.[1]

The borderline patient, then, is at all times potentially tormented by such anxieties, which he must constantly face. One of his possible ways of dealing with them is sexualization, which gives rise to pleasure.[2] This defence can lead to temporary compromises that may neutralize anxiety, but it involves further imbalances that facilitate the emergence of psychotic states.

Borderline patients typically exhibit a fluidity of personal identity and in regard to the positions of aggression or submission. This makes them more amenable to change and more receptive to psychoanalytic help than subjects with structured perversions.

Here are some examples.

A patient in analysis was going through a crisis that repeated the experience of infantile anxiety following the death of his mother, who had been his only positive point of reference. At this time the patient was tormented by anxiety-inducing visions in which he felt threatened by his father, with whom he fantasized a sexual encounter in which he experienced pleasure at being sodomized. This enabled him to keep at bay the anxiety aroused by the prospect of being killed.

On another occasion the same patient dreamed that a vampire was chasing him, intent on sucking his brains out, and that he tried to placate him by offering his penis instead. The vampire masturbated his penis, thus transforming the terror into a pleasurable experience.

What is significant in these two clinical fragments is the attempt to introduce the traumatic anxieties into the sensual world, with a view to modifying them by a sexualized confusion between aggressor and victim.

In another case, however, the coexistence of persecutory anxieties and a perverse excitation is obvious. The patient concerned had constructed a masturbatory world of sexualized violence. He would sometimes dress up as a Nazi officer and, standing in front of a mirror, would have fantasies of sadistically penetrating or torturing a pre-pubescent young man, who would in turn be aroused. The token of the boy's arousal was an erection in the patient, whose penis represented the tortured boy. This fantasy of violence was usually accompanied by excitation and orgasm.

Sometimes, however, the consequence was anxiety at the possibility of retaliatory violence.

For instance, this patient once dreamed of a white shark that was caught by a fisherman. The fish was torn to pieces, its bones protruding through the lacerations in its body, but the fisherman refused to give it the *coup de grâce* because he wanted to take it home alive and eat it fresh. The patient's associations showed that the shark represented the healthy and voracious libidinal self. The sadism was the man's, because he was aroused by the idea of devouring living flesh.

It is interesting to note that, when this patient had fantasies of sadomasochistic actions, he did not experience them as cruel, because the erotic excitation caused him to lose contact with pain and fear and with the distinction between persecutor and victim. In the dream, however, because the patient perceived the distinction between the persecutor (the fisherman) and the victim (the shark), he became aware of painful emotions and cruelty. Although in a state of impotence, the infantile self succeeded in perceiving the cruelty of the situation, and thus felt anxious and tormented.

The mixture of terror and states of sexualization suggests that an excess of persecutory anxieties might be a contributory factor to perversion. Alongside the terror, there develops a sexualized aggressive pleasure; this transformation allows the subject to abolish the perception of fear and steers excitation towards the exaltation of violence.

It may be postulated that perverse borderlines needed, as children, to sexualize excessive anxiety by transforming it into excitation. Identification with the persecutor turns the terrified child into a sadistic adult.

Genetic hypotheses swing between two positions: in the first, the child is left excessively alone with his death anxieties (death being seen as continuous persecution); while, in the second, the child is removed from the parents and cultivates secret fantasies in which the suffering inflicted becomes exciting.

As we have seen, the patient may identify either with the willing, sexualized victim or with the sadistic aggressor—or with both. If he succeeds in preserving the distinction between the good self and the bad object, he may perceive himself as a persecuted victim in whom the (defensive) sexual pleasure is mixed with the fear of annihilation. If, however, he loses the ability to make this distinction and evil becomes good and exciting, the perception of pain is erased. In the latter case, the pleasure stems from the assumption of the negative identity of the persecutor and from the fantasy of the victim's consenting submission.

In borderline perversion, the good self becomes the passive self; the infantile part is incapable of escaping from the fascination of the destructive power, and this submission permits an internal agreement between the sadistic parent and the ill-treated child.

In an interesting paper entitled "The mirror: a perverse sexual fantasy in a woman, seen as a defence against a psychotic breakdown", Riesenberg Malcolm (1969) describes a female patient whose psychotic parts were encapsulated in a perverse syndrome that enabled the rest of her personality to establish a modicum of contact with reality and to preserve a minimum of normal functioning. The perversion is said to have been established as a protection against falling to pieces.

In the period before her stay in a psychiatric hospital, when she had engaged in constant sexual promiscuity, the patient had constructed a complex fantasy of a "one-way mirror" behind which all kinds of sexual activities involving violent or explicitly sadistic encounters took place. Each participant had to perform humiliating acts and often had incestuous sexual relations. Although these lasted a long time, there were numerous obstacles to the achievement of pleasure; cruelty was frequently the predominant factor. The patient felt that she "was" each of the characters, or "was inside" them.

While all these things were going on behind the mirror, a large number of spectators were watching from the outside. They were frequently aroused by what they saw in the mirror and had to resist this arousal—for if they succumbed to it, they were dragged inside the mirror. Once inside, they had to find a partner, because sexual coupling was *de rigueur* there.

The author contends that the mirror fantasy represented an attempt, using perverse means, to reconstruct the patient's parental couple and her own ego. The mirror became a structure in which the most disturbed aspects were encapsulated and contained in strictly delimited spaces. The parents were represented by the participants in the scenes taking place within the mirror. The purpose of the entire operation was to provide the ego with the minimum conditions for survival, but it was carried out in such circumstances of cruelty, hate and humiliation that the loving impulses were evidently pervaded with destructiveness. The sadism was never allowed to be modified by love and had to be constantly gratified to ensure that no approach to integration took place.

Beyond the dynamic significance attributed by the author to the perverse process, it is interesting to note that the perverse fantasy took the place of the acted-out state of sexualization that had preceded the analysis and resulted in the patient's hospitalization. During her psychoanalytic treatment the danger persisted and was represented by the possibility of being captured by a sexualized psychotic part, described in the voyeuristic and perverse fantasy, when the spectator was attracted and in turn drawn into the mirror. The mirror thus represented the sexualized mental state with the power to attract the watcher: before her admission to hospital, the patient herself had tried to enter a convent as a defence against the urge to indulge in sexual promiscuity.

As the author points out, the variation in the number of spectators constituting the audience on the outside of the mirror was a measure of the greater or lesser availability of the patient's healthy parts; however, their existence on the outside could not contribute in any way to change, because they were powerless to alter anything. The spectators corresponded to the voyeuristic and arousable parts of the patient.

Perversion and psychosis

Conflicting views have been expressed on the relationship between perversion and psychosis, according to the theories to which the relevant authors subscribe.

Glover (1933, 1964) suggests that perversion preserves the patient's reality sense, protecting him from the psychosis that threatens to invade his personality.

This view was overturned by subsequent psychoanalytic research. With the contribution of the post-Kleinian authors, the concept of perversion was seen as coinciding with a pathological form of relationship between different parts of the psyche. Contrary to Glover's hypothesis, the perverse organization of the mind was now seen as a transitional or aggregational stage on the path to psychosis.

In a paper published in 1982, Betty Joseph identifies certain areas of psychic experience that she describes as "addiction to near death", which are manifested during the therapy of patients who, while not otherwise particularly deprived or frustrated as small children, had withdrawn into a secret world of violence. This violence, mentally and physically sexualized in masturbatory fashion, is seen as coinciding with a withdrawal in which the body is the place where the omnipotence of the sadomasochistic fantasy is preserved. Submission to pleasure abolishes the perception of pain and ensures the continuity of the sadomasochistic vicious circle.

The study of the sadomasochistic perversion helps to throw light on the mysterious phenomenon of pleasure in self-destruction, which links the world of perversion to that of psychosis. For in psychosis, as in perversion, masturbatory excitation involves a state of omnipotent domination of the body and of the mind. Another common aspect is transgression, with its twofold connotation of violence and subversion.

The inner descent into psychosis begins with an attack on the subject's own psychic functioning, which is subverted; psychic reality can be transformed, and anything can be changed into its opposite. By altering the order of perceptions, the subject can condition his own senses so as to modify the sense of reality and abolish the perception of doubt.

The psychotic patient is fascinated by this "perversity", which coincides with a transgressive destruction of thought whereby dream, delusion and reality are no longer distinguished. There is a strong resemblance between the psychotic patient, who creates an omnipotent reality in which he can do anything he pleases, and the perverse patient, who creates a world in which he can subvert the symbolic order of human relations.

During an episode of psychotic excitation occurring in the course of his analysis, a young male patient described his mental state in a dream: "I was invited by a couple of analysts to their home. I got into their double bed and started whirling my body about. I felt intense sensual pleasure because I could do anything I wanted. The figures of my parents appeared, far off and washed out. Suddenly the pleasure turned into anxiety. I was surrounded by lots and lots of small animals like little basset hounds, deformed and with their heads bent back, complaining and accusing me of being responsible for their deformity".

The dream described the sexualized excitation (the double bed) accompanying the psychotic state, and the sense of omnipotence that followed the perception of the intrusive transgression. The attack on the parents subsequently proved to be an attack on the patient's own mind, which was damaged by it (he said that the little dogs were parts of himself).

Like psychotic transgression, perverse transgression has to do with subverting the organization of the internal affective world, which gives rise to a sexualized pleasure.

The clinical data show that in both psychosis and perversion, the body may become a place where the subject can isolate himself from the world, as well as a means of internal production of sensuality and perceptual omnipotence.

In my paper on psychic strategies of self-annihilation (De Masi, 1996), I described the self-induced state of pleasure that accompanies certain regressive experiences based on perverse and self-destructive psychic processes which are not perceived as such and betoken the entry into psychosis.

Psychic regression and pleasure come together to subvert loving relationships (in perversions) and the organizing function of thought and affects (in psychosis). The difference is that the psychotic patient has to face the persecutory sense of guilt, whereas the perverse patient can remain immune from it and escape anxiety.

Criminality and perversion

Psychoanalytic literature includes a considerable body of material on criminality and perversion, on the connections between them and on what distinguishes them from each other. One current thesis is that in criminality destructiveness is manifested in the pure state, whereas in perversion it is bound and mitigated by sexuality.

The observation that the perverse subject usually obtains his partner's consent for the aggressive game has led to the belief that love or sexual interest reduces the desire to harm. The agreement between the sadistic perpetrator of violence and the masochistic victim is enshrined in the contract concluded between the two, so that the voluntary submission of the passive partner limits the extent of the damage. In perverse criminality, conversely, the attacker acts against, and independently of, his victim.

According to another interpretation, the differences between perversion and criminality are quantitative only: perversion is a private fact that becomes public, and hence criminal, when the sexual act is acted out and causes harm falling within the legal definition of a punishable offence.

I shall now describe a perversion which gradually turned into actual criminal behaviour, and which may be regarded as evidence in favour of the second hypothesis. The description is taken from the notes of the social worker in charge of Jürgen Bartsch, whose case is described in Miller's *For Your Own Good* (1980).

After a number of failed attempts, Jürgen Bartsch finally succeeded in killing four youths aged between 16 and 20. Even if each crime varied in detail, the basic procedure was always the same: having lured the youth into an old air-raid shelter, Jürgen would beat him, terrorize him into a totally submissive state, tie him up, manipulate his genitals and finally strangle him or beat him to death.

Although Jürgen himself and the doctors who surgically castrated him believed the contrary, sexuality seems to have had little to do with the motivation of his criminal acts.

Jürgen confessed that, from the age of 13 or 14, his mind had been increasingly disturbed, so that he was ultimately powerless to influence the events that were to overwhelm him. For a long time he prayed, hoping that this at least might be of some help. He reported that he was particularly aroused by the dazed eyes of his victims: paralysed with terror, these young men became so small and submissive that they were unable to protest or defend themselves in any way. The victims' helplessness inflamed the aggressor's sadism even more.

According to the detailed description given to the court, the acme of excitation was attained not during masturbation, but only when the victim's body was cut. This meticulous operation gave rise to a kind of permanent mental orgasm. There is not enough information to reconstruct the progressive and inexorable seizure of power by the sadistic, murderous part over the rest of Jürgen's personality. Since feelings of friendship and brotherhood for his young companions persisted in other parts of his person, he must surely have struggled to rein in and neutralize the perverse part of himself. Ultimately, however, just as his victims appeared submissive and incapable of defence, so the good part of his personality became totally helpless and colluded with the murderous part.

This case history presented by Miller, despite the summary nature of the autobiographical account, confirms that—in some cases at least—the achievement of lustful mental pleasure underlies the criminal impulse.

Jürgen's testimony again suggests continuity between perversion and criminal sexuality. We do not know why the acting out of cruelty and the infliction of suffering give rise to orgasmic mental excitation. We can only record the fact that the link with sexual ecstasy makes cruelty increasingly devastating and dangerous. This type of pleasure seems totally detached from the sexual act and the associated gratification (libido), and is therefore inconsistent with the Freudian paradigm. Destructiveness triumphs through the criminal act because such an act can trigger this type of pleasure.

My example falls more within the category of a criminal perversion than in that of sexual criminality proper. In the latter, the victim is a hated object, the killing of whom gives rise to pleasure. When the victim is a woman, she is experienced as a rejecting narcissistic object. The sexual crime is committed in revenge for an excessively persistent humiliation: having sexually abused his victim, the criminal kills her. He retains memories, body parts or items of personal clothing as trophies.

None of this is seen in sexual perversion. On reflection, we find that the sadomasochistic perversion usually coincides not with the "pleasure of doing evil", but with the excitation that accompanies the perverse act and fantasy. The master in the sadomasochistic game derives sexual pleasure from the fact that the servant does everything he wants, and not from any hatred of him. The structured perversion is relatively benign not because of the docility of the perverse subject but because of the absence of destructive hate or envy of the victim. The pervert loves cruelty, but does not hate his victim.

However, in perversion too, a dangerous escalation, intimately connected with the nature of the perverse excitation and pleasure, must be kept under control. Even if the extreme positions are never fully attained in perversion, but kept within the play of the imagination, the perverse subject nevertheless often pushes himself to the limit with a view to achieving an ever more voluptuous orgasm. Since sexual excitation arises out of the omnipotent idea of having the partner totally in one's power, the determinant of pleasure tends to shift increasingly towards the wish to have the subjugated victim totally at the pervert's disposal.

Although not due to hate, murder becomes desirable in so far as it coincides with a maximum of transgressive licence and omnipotence: "Anything is permitted, even killing!" Extreme fantasies may be enjoyed by the use of recorded pornographic material, which establishes the appropriate distance between the subject and actual crime.

Other factors are involved in the process of escalation. One of the most important, in my view, is habituation, which results in a raising of the threshold of pleasure. The stimulus shifts towards a heightening of sadism, and correspondingly of masochism, through images and, where possible, actions. For this reason, as in the case of drug addiction, the "daily dose" of the "noxa" must be constantly increased.

A literary demonstration of the above can be found in Sade's "One hundred and twenty days of Sodom" (1784). The protagonist's orgasm can be kept at its peak only through a constant intensification of the level of abuse and violence. Sexual cruelty is practised first on the predestined victim and then on the libertines' assistants and collaborators. In this way, the initially refined, methodical and ironic sexual abuse ultimately becomes pure murderous violence.

In the final pages, at the point when the libertines really do have their victims wholly at their disposal, Sade presents the issue of habituation. Durcet, one of the protagonists, wonders whether he and his companions really are having pleasure. Happiness cannot consist in satisfying one's desires at will; the missing element is pleasure in the prohibited and, in particular, the spectacle of the unhappy people who are deprived of pleasure. This results from the comparison of one's own pleasure with the unhappiness of others: an excess of pleasure is secured only by accentuating the suffering of others. The libertines know that they owe their own erections to their commission of evil acts, and not to the objects themselves.

For this reason, crime exerts a special fascination. Durcet confesses that he has dreamed infinitely more of what he has never been able to do, and has always had to complain that Nature, in giving him a taste for offending Nature itself, has deprived him of the means to do so. Curval, another libertine, agrees: there are only two or three kinds of crime and, once these have been committed, it is all over. The utmost offence would be to attack the sun so as to abolish the universe and really to destroy the world; that would be a genuine crime, and not a series of wretched misdeeds!

Hence the possible escalation of perversion into a criminal act results from factors inherent in the nature and dynamics of perverse pleasure, and not from hate for an object.

The perverse individual necessarily commits his crimes in the world of fantasy and fiction. So it was, to some extent, for Sade himself: while in prison or criminal asylum in which he was confined on account of his sexual excesses and the persecution of the authorities, he was able to give his incessant perverse fantasies concrete form by describing them in novels, so that the horror was contained in the uncanny fascination of his literary oeuvre.

Notes

1. Freud describes the hypnotic power of anxiety in "The 'uncanny'" (1919h).
2. Erotized submission and passivity have long been investigated by psychoanalysis. In a later consideration of Freud's Wolf Man case, Klein disagrees with Freud's hypothesis of the masochistic submission of the patient, identified with his mother in intercourse with the father, and contends that the patient was made anxious by the father and terrified by him. In her view, the erotized submission stems not from love but from the patient's attempt to defend himself and thereby to placate the persecutor.

CHAPTER ELEVEN

Infantile trauma and perversion

A psychic trauma is an action, either sudden or repeated, that proves harmful because the defences required to protect the individual who undergoes it are not yet ready. It is typical of the traumatic situation that the subject is confronted by a crushing event that cannot be understood or coped with mentally.

Infancy, of course, is the time of greatest exposure. When the trauma is occasioned by the child's care-givers—e.g. the parents—the harmful effect is greater.

Views differ on the significance of early infantile traumatic experiences in the development of the pathologies or forms of suffering that will later emerge in adulthood. The uncertainty begins with the type of experience to be seen as traumatic in any individual case. An appraisal perhaps may be possible only retrospectively.

The systematic administration of beatings or humiliations has lasting adverse effects on the victim's personality. An ill-treated child may develop a state of evacuation or masochistic passivity or, conversely, may readily, by identification, turn into a sadistic aggressor. There is a great deal of evidence that abused children become violent parents when they grow up.

Both masochistic passivity and sadistic violence due to infantile traumas must be distinguished from sexual perversion. Glenn (1984) reports on the cases of three patients who underwent major surgery in infancy and subsequently developed erotized sadomasochistic fantasies. In these cases, masochism constitutes a repetitive, compulsive formation that can be indirectly linked to the original trauma, but which never becomes a sadomasochistic structure proper.

Similar observations were made by Stoller (1975) in adult patients. The panel "Sadomasochism in children" (Panel, 1985) includes a number of reports of: (1) premature babies who underwent traumatic surgery; (2) families in which adults plainly abused children; (3) games played by children who had been sexually abused; and (4) the therapy of abused children (Grossman, 1991). In all these cases, the children developed an appreciable capacity for attracting aggression and for practising aggression themselves.

These dramatic case histories demonstrate that very young infants are extraordinarily inclined to react to trauma by behaviour destructive of self and others. Partial assimilation of the traumatic experience depends very largely on the response of the child's adult care-givers. For this reason, the relationship between early trauma and subsequent development is a complex one.

Although these studies tell us a great deal about the development of aggressive and destructive behaviour, they fail to establish a manifest link between trauma and the sadomasochistic perversion. Psychoanalytic clinical experience, for its part, confirms that, while traumatic experiences in infancy may facilitate entry into perversion, many perverts were adequately protected in infancy.

Even so, some analysts have put forward a traumatic theory of perversion in which the idea of trauma differs from the ordinary conception of a violent harmful action. For these authors, the trauma consists in the psychological pressure, whether seductive or authoritarian, that may be exerted by the adult (usually the mother) on the child's mind, thereby attacking his perception of independence and separateness and his sense of personal and sexual identity.

The hypotheses advanced by Stoller (1975) are plausible, but, as stated earlier, a link between infantile traumas and the development of perversion cannot easily be demonstrated in every instance of perversion.

The infantile microtraumas subsumed by Khan (1979) in the concept of cumulative trauma may help to create certain narcissistic and autoerotic areas in the character, but do not seem to be specific to the development of perversion in adulthood. Some authors, on the other hand, consider that perversions result from an infantile "withdrawal" due to the emotional remoteness of the parents. This kind of interpretation applies to the case described by Joseph in "Addiction to near death" (1982).

The trauma–perversion sequence may be reversed: in children secretly given to sadomasochistic pleasure, traumatic experiences may stimulate sexualization. In these cases trauma, rather than being seen as a source of anxiety, may rekindle the sadistic pleasure and mobilize the masochistic fantasy.

The relationship between trauma and perversion remains open to other evaluations; there is a need for further clinical material whereby the relative weight of family factors and internal personality dynamics may emerge more clearly. However, while it should be borne in mind that a perversion can develop even in the absence of verifiable traumas, there is in my opinion no "normality" in the pervert's family environment. Very often we find that the parents are totally indifferent to the child's psychic withdrawal, in which the perversion is secretly maturing.

Besides physical aggression like beatings or sadistic acts, a child may be exposed to sexual traumas, such as episodic or continued instances of sexual violence and repeated sexual stimulation. A child who is the object of adult sexual attentions may engage early on in processes of sexualization, which pave the way to perverse experiences. Children from debased family backgrounds who are exposed to prolonged sexual manipulation from regressed or psychotic parents reproduce these manifestations in sexualized approaches to their psychotherapists (Gluckman, 1987).

Even if aggressive or sexual traumas can be identified in the history of certain patients, a direct correlation between these and perversion cannot be established. A child who is sexually abused by an adult undergoes a catastrophic attack on his trust in the world, which undermines his capacity to believe in dependence on human objects. Sexual abuse is surely the most serious form of adult betrayal of a child (Parens, 1997).

More than a century on from Freud's first intuitions, the recent abundance of psychoanalytic publications, mostly by American authors (typified by the contributions in *Psychoanalytic Inquiry* 17(3), 1998, a monograph on sexual abuse), shows on the basis of clinical accounts that sexual trauma distorts the development of a child, causing him to forget the traumatic experience and making him unable to understand it. Sexual trauma and seduction by adults induce the child to confront the processes of growth by an emotional dissociation intended to erase the experience of abuse (Davies, 1996).

Sexual traumas often underlie sexual inhibitions, frigidity or masochistic fantasies. By preventing the development of the capacity for pleasure, the trauma opens the way to masochistic pleasure: the passive victim can now obtain active pleasure. In some women, the frigidity resulting from infantile sexual abuse can be circumvented by the mobilization of self-annihilation fantasies. These, however, are manoeuvres aimed at achieving orgasm in normal sexual intercourse, and not instances of perversion proper.

According to Novick & Novick (1996), masochistic children with stubborn beating fantasies, unlike adolescents with episodic symptoms, will always have had emotional difficulties in the first months of their lives. The lack of mutual pleasure in the mother–child relationship is a constant in psychoanalytic treatment. In the case of non-sexual traumas, there is a common tendency to recreate the painful events through identification with the aggressor or to revive them by defensive erotization.

In recent psychoanalytic studies, the concept of trauma has been widened and given a more extensive meaning: anything that cannot be elaborated psychically or symbolically is deemed traumatic. Beyond Khan's conception of cumulative trauma, the epithet "traumatic" is now applied to the situation described by Ferenczi (1949) concerning the suffering induced in infants by systematic incomprehension on the part of adults. The concept of trauma is now seen more in a relational context than in terms of a chance external factor acting on a specific area. Abuse may be psychologically traumatic, injuring the sense of trust in "self in the world"—that is, the potential area that enables the subject to feel in harmony with others, to have wishes, and to project himself into life by way of a personal space and imagination filled with a dense network of thoughts and emotions.

When a child feels consistently repudiated and denied in his thoughts and qualities, his entire emotional system suffers in consequence. The child must reconcile the desired experience of a good parent with the actual, unconscious reality of not having had his love acknowledged. An adolescent or adult seemingly capable of efficient functioning may become structured around a wounded child deprived of a shared emotional world (Zerbi Schwartz, 1998). Beneath this adult, however, there often lurks a person who lacks a free and trusting emotional and relational field. The traumatic experience, which has never been consciously worked through, has made it impossible for the subject to perceive himself as a whole person.

Family relationships, where unequivocally pathological, are also damaging. In the case of a girl, the experience of seeing the parents engaged in sadomasochistic collusion (the mother apparently consenting to be dominated by a sexually abusing husband) reinforces her idea of a sadistic penis and an unequal relationship. She gains impression that the sexual encounter takes place without mutual pleasure or for the pleasure of one partner only. If this is the emotional world of the little girl, it is easy to imagine the nature of her later adult sexual experience.

Sexuality experienced as traumatic in infancy does not kindle desire. When a woman with this background is in a sexual situation, she will not succeed in attaining orgasm, for that demands freedom and total trust in the partner. For her this is impossible. The partner is unconsciously experienced as the intrusive, psychologically and physically violent father. Sexual desire, being devoid of any affective component, is experienced as bad and degrading.

Personal pleasure is not allowed; the woman can experience it at most as a reflection of the other's pleasure. It is impossible to achieve orgasm in unison, although sometimes it can be obtained solitarily or after actual intercourse.

The preconditions for the emergence of the sadomasochistic fantasy can be identified precisely in this context. If there has been a trauma, whether psychic or physical, it is possible for the submissive condition to be sexualized. In this way the patient can identify with the figure undergoing the coitus of an aggressive male. The figure of the partner cannot be experienced as an object of positive cathexes and desires.

In some cases the real experience of coitus is dissociated from the self and projected into the vision of the partner's union with another woman. This permits an excitation in which no guilt attaches to sexual desire because the pleasure belongs to another.

It is impossible to experience orgasm in sexual intercourse with the partner, but only through masochistic or voyeuristic fantasies. In all these cases of seeming frigidity, it is found that the lack of a good internalized relationship has prevented the development of the sexual imagination that arises out of the infantile pre-conception of a good relationship between the parents. These female patients cannot experience sexual pleasure because they are unable to explore and project pleasurable desires. The masochistic fantasy harks back to the psychic or physical trauma that has impressed its stamp on the delicate, sensitive area of sexuality.

These forms of masochism plainly differ from perversion, in which the masochistic fantasy is an expedient for achieving the orgasm that cannot otherwise be obtained. The underlying suffering has to do with a mortified self, deprived of value, which cannot be the subject of desire. My psychoanalytic experience suggests that this type of suffering is present particularly in women with depressive tendencies. In my view, infantile psychic trauma is a major cause of areas of suffering in adult love life, and underlies many forms of female sexual masochism.

In men, too, a traumatic infancy may, if the subject has not yet become aware of and assimilated it as such, be connected with areas of sexual inhibition accompanied by perverse disturbances of sexuality. A married young man asked for psychoanalytic help on account of a complex set of phobic-anxiety symptoms and a work inhibition. He recalled a childhood overshadowed by his mother's alcoholism: whereas she would sometimes beat him savagely, once sober she would then express her unconditional devotion to him. The young patient remained heavily dependent on this mother and showed a formal respect for social conventions and human relations. In fact, however, his internal world was empty. His love for his wife was more like a state of devoted submission, since he had never been able to feel intimately bound to her. He claimed to have no passionate feelings for anyone. Alternating between submission and flight, he knew that the strength of his desires drew him cyclically into "areas of freedom", involving frenetic sexual encounters with prostitutes or transvestites, in which he often derived sexual pleasure from putting himself in a position of masochistic excitation. The idea that "you can do anything you want" drove him into states of bodily and mental arousal tantamount to experiences of depersonalization, which relieved him of the burden of being himself. These sexual encounters strongly resembled alcoholic binges. Of course, the attempt to solve his problems by excitation meant that he was never able to overcome his state of chronic lack of vitality and personal freedom.

CHAPTER TWELVE

Final notes on the three paradigms

J ust as the sexual deviations are very diverse psychic experiences that cannot readily be subsumed under a single common denominator, so too the sadomasochistic sexual perversion cannot be classified under one heading owing to its multiplicity of levels and psychodynamic implications.

Of all the perversions, this one (in which the polymorphism of symptoms is an expression of different kinds of mental suffering) is surely the most complex and difficult to interpret. Sexual sadomasochism, after all, may be the outcome of infantile traumas, but also of a climate of excessive affective coldness or distance in the environment of the growing child. Finally, perverse mental states, whether temporary or permanent, may be observed in borderline pathology, in certain psychotic experiences, or in criminal acts.

Understandably, given the often complex and contradictory clinical data (one need only think of the significance of trauma), the various analytic models have had to simplify the complexity of the subject, blurring certain aspects and emphasizing others. It seems to me that this is the price to be paid by all authors who have sought to formulate a general theory of the perversions. I also believe that the various models refer to differing mental states or psychopathological structures.

Note that, because the three paradigms (see Chapter 8) take the form of finished and self-referring theories, they can be specifically compared only by constant reference to the general theory that underlies them and to their component parts. Although each paradigm includes valuable elements for understanding the complex world of perversion, none appears exhaustive.

Psychoanalysis owes the discovery of infantile sexuality to the perversions, and these, in turn, owe much to the theory of psychosexuality. Today, however, Freud's theories of infantile sexuality no longer constitute the linchpin of interpretations of the perversions, but have been replaced by some of his later intuitions on the general principles of mental functioning. I hope that this book will illustrate the route leading from Freud's first formulations to our present views—a route that has benefited from the contributions of many authors, inspired by a variety of theories and models, all of them important and worthy of integration within a pluralistic vision reflecting different observational vantage points.

I shall now attempt to compare my own conception of perversion, which I hope will have emerged from the above exposition, with the current models, with a view to showing how much of each formulation has been superseded and how much retains its validity.

My basic conception is that perversion is a *technique of mental excitation* which arises out of isolation and is pursued in the personal *imagination*. The excitation is self-generated through certain specific configurations centring on the pleasure of dominating or possessing another or, conversely, of being dominated or abused. Even if the sphere of action in perversion is confined to that of sexuality, the excitation stems not from the primitive form of sexuality but rather from the idea of power, without which no perverse sexuality would ever be mobilized.

The sadomasochistic perversion in particular is underlain by a fantasy prepared in infancy—a nucleus around which the subject more and more exclusively prepares the imaginative movements that lead to the sadomasochistic orgasm.

Hence the importance assumed by infantile sexuality in perversion—a concept that is in turn complex and riddled with contradictions. Without wishing to deny the role of sensuality and the search for pleasure in infancy, I should like to distinguish sexuality in the child from the sexualized child. As stated earlier, the experience of *sexualization* consists in a technique of transformation of perceptions whereby a particular kind of orgasmic pleasure can be obtained. It is a pleasure arising out of an anti-relational sexuality—an expansion of the mind produced by the imagination. The child may resort to sexualization following an environmental facilitation, for example if stimulated by the erotic attentions of adults, or on account of a particular personal excitability.

The situation is at any rate one of *early withdrawal*—what Steiner (1993) calls a psychic retreat—in which the sexualized pleasure obtained by masturbatory techniques becomes the pole of development and attraction. In the sadomasochistic perversion, strength of character is weakened from the earliest years of life by submission to the pleasure of bad behaviour, whereby children, even if they seemingly develop and acquire operational capabilities, preserve a relational and affective world distorted by the erotized fascination of power. The conquest of the mind by the perverse pleasure—a mixture of excitation and indifference—replaces relational hate and aggression. The child therefore fails to develop a vital rage towards bad objects, but instead fears and idolizes them. The part of the personality that feeds on sadomasochistic fantasies consciously coexists with that which remains in contact with the affective world.

The perverse subject possesses a twofold logic and moral system: the values that function and are venerated in the perverse system are not those of the healthy part.

I agree with Freud's view that the sadomasochistic fantasy is primarily sadistic. To obtain the maximum pleasure in triumph, the sadist constructs the compliant masochistic object in his imagination. Before being attracted by masochism, the masochist has experienced sadistic pleasure.

Once the figure of the masochist has been constructed in fantasy, the sadist can enjoy the perversion of his counterpart; in this way the sadomasochistic solution constantly satisfies all possible requirements. The *sadomasochistic monad* basically coincides with the maximum of narcissistic performance: the object accedes in every respect to the other's pleasure and will. For this reason, the subject's own body, the subjugated and controllable docile pleasure object, becomes the most suitable setting for the perverse fantasy. Because sexual pleasure has the characteristics of mental lust, I postulate that perverse pleasure tends to subjugate the rest of the personality, in a *dynamic similar to that of drugged enslavement*. The fact that the perverse subject depends on sexuality to produce an addictive type of orgasm means that he has thereby found a way of achieving drugged ecstasy.

If we call into question the existence of a continuum between ordinary and perverse sexuality, we must necessarily reconsider the legitimacy of classifying the perversions as a disturbance of sexual behaviour. The fact that sexuality is one of the means of achieving pleasure and that perversion resorts to sexuality, albeit of a special, drugged kind, suggests that this classification is inappropriate.

My own theory replaces the traditional concept of aggression by that of destructiveness, understood as the fantasy of domination of the object that constitutes the stimulus for excitation. Perversion offers the experience of a paradisiacal pleasure whereby anything seems possible.

In its various forms and degrees of structuring, the sadomaso- chistic perversion may be seen as the erotized variant of the psychotic part of the personality. By way of the sexualization of domination, the world of omnipotence exalts the pathological mixture that makes the destructive drives ever more virulent.

There is in my view no strict correlation between infantile traumas or microtraumas and the development of the sadomasochistic perversion. It seems to me that perversion proper develops by way of a particular propensity to withdraw into an exciting fantasy world associated with split-off aggressive rivalry and greed satisfied in the imagination. Another facilitating factor must surely be parental compliance. It is easier for adults who were themselves ill-treated or abused children to develop states of evacuation and passivity or to identify with aggressors of the past, in turn becoming agents of violence or abuse, but not necessarily sexual perverts.

The relationship between perversion and suffering is another matter. Whereas it can be shown that destructive pleasure some- times assumes the meaning of a desperate response to unbearable pain, I do not believe that this is the case in perversion.

In the last chapter of *Martin Eden*, Jack London describes the precise sequence of thoughts that accompany the hero as he commits suicide. In the process of drowning, Eden experiences a contemptuous triumph over the part of himself that would like to survive. In the novel, this state of mind stems from the despair that overwhelms the hero when, having achieved literary success, he realizes that the hopes and ideals of friendship for the achievement of which he has suffered intensely have been destroyed by reality. In his case, masochistic rage is turned against the suffering self; the suffering stimulates a punitive superego, which produces a dramatic self-destructive masochism. The attack is directed towards the perceptuo–emotional part of the self, which is felt to be the source of the pain.

Perversion is remote from this self-destructive pain; it is not a paradoxical, catastrophic defence against pain and despair. The physical pain experienced is not synonymous with suffering. The enslavement and brutalization of the subject's own body gives pleasure—a primary pleasure in destruction.

I shall now examine some of the traditional positions maintained within the various relevant theoretical orientations and attempt to answer the particular questions they raise.

Perversion as an outcome of infantile sexuality

Should the first theoretical paradigm, which sees the sadomasochistic perversion as the aggressive form of infantile love, continue to be upheld? As late as in 1973, the *International Journal of Psycho-Analysis* presented a paper, by Stolorow & Grand, in which perversion was explained by this theory.

A 25-year-old patient with a masochistic personality had a rare perversion. He would walk along the street holding a bug in his hand. On seeing a woman, he would deposit the bug on the back of the unfortunate victim, who would be terrified, throw it to the ground and crush it underfoot. The patient became aroused on seeing the creature squashed; back home, he would then masturbate while reliving the scene. He connected the idea of the bug being squashed with a memory of the excitation he had experienced when being spanked by his mother, and of his mother's excitation while spanking him. From a very early age he had felt excited when his mother went after flies; the excitation was proportional to the sadistic pleasure his mother derived from this action. The perversion seemed to be maintained by a fixation on to the anal–sadistic and masochistic components of infantile sexuality. The patient was identified with the sadistic mother squashing the bug, as well as, masochistically, with the bug being squashed. His castration anxiety, as a result of which he could not look at the female genitals without terror, could therefore be interpreted as follows: it was better to have a penis-as-bug-squashed-by-a-woman than for it to be cut off by the vagina (dentata); a flaccid penis was preserved from castration.

On rereading the contributions of authors who subscribe to the libido theory, one cannot escape the impression that this model tends to "flatten" the perversion by presenting it in terms of the already known—namely, infantile sexuality and castration anxiety. The latter in particular, the cornerstone of the entire theoretical edifice, ultimately becomes an excessively generic interpretative key.

In the three decades following the publication of Freud's last essay on perversion ("Fetishism", 1927e), no original work appeared to complement his oeuvre except for Glover's 1933 paper mentioned earlier.

The contribution of the second-generation analysts was confined to confirming the psychosexual theory and making it definitive, by means of a conspicuously large number of published case histories.

This is evident from the book by Lorand & Balint (1956), in whose compilation all the scientific papers, however varied and interesting (the authors include Gillespie, Alexander, Bychowsky, Grunberger, Bak, Lacan, and Granoff), belong to the first paradigm, whether the subject is fetishism, exhibitionism, sadomasochism, homosexuality or some other manifestation.

The main tenets of this theory, such as a stoppage of development due to an aggravation of primitive components, or the concept of regression (to the anal–sadistic stage), suggest a permeability between the stages of psychosexual development which portrays the transition from perverse to relational sexuality as easier than clinical reality shows it to be. Again, the stoppage in development featuring in this model tends to undervalue the effect of the split-off sexualized nucleus that is operational and endowed with seductive capacities, which can progressively damage the rest of the personality.

The hypothesis that perversion has its origins in polymorphous infantile sexuality turns out to be not only insufficient for an understanding of sadomasochism, but also not easily reconcilable with the subsequent contributions by Freud himself on the three types of masochism, the masturbation fantasy and the theory of the fusion and defusion of the life and death drives.

Continuity of normal and perverse sexuality

The psychosexual theory, which implies a continuum between normality and perversion, distinguishes the existence of a physiological propensity to perversion from perversion proper. I take issue with the view that the two forms preserve genetic links but diverge in terms of degree and exclusiveness.

In the theories that invoke psychosexuality, the possible superimposition of different semantic levels makes for a wide field of discretion that leads to eclecticism.

The word "libido" is used in the theory in many different senses that ought to be distinguished: for instance, it may denote infantile sensuality, excitation and physical discharge, sexual pleasure, pleasure in the encounter with the object, object love, and so on. When the notion of the "sexual continuum" is expanded, paradoxical conclusions inevitably result.

Kernberg (1995) investigates the dynamic of sexual excitation and erotic desire precisely on the basis of the concepts of the psychosexual theory. He considers that sexual excitation includes the capacity to bind aggression to sexual libidinal elements; sadism and masochism are inherent in the wishes for symbiotic fusion, penetration and bisexual identification that are typical of erotic desires.

In Kernberg's view, the subject's wish to transgress the Oedipal prohibitions and to violate the secrecy of the primal scene, by imposing himself on an object that denies itself, entails the same aggression as does perversion. This author sees every sexual gratification as the expression of unconscious fantasies that include sadistic, masochistic, exhibitionistic and voyeuristic elements. Defining sadomasochistic perversion as a generically aggressive act, he arrives at a solution, which is brilliant in theory but does not stand up to clinical scrutiny, according to which ordinary and perverse sexual excitation are substantially the same. In his opinion, there is a surprising resemblance between the aggression of perversion and that of normal love relations. In a couple relationship, aggression is expressed in sadistic or masochistic activities, and in the use of the partner as a subordinated sexual object; sexual excitation includes an element of unconditional surrender and acceptance of a state of slavery. Kernberg points out that sadomasochism is not only a pathology confined to perverse subjects, but also an essential component of sexual behaviour and fantasy. He considers that sexual excitation at its highest pitch approaches the fantasy world of perversion and pornography. This aspect makes sexual play an erotic art—unlike pornography, which is repetitive and mechanical.

My own view is that, even if there are superficial analogies with certain perversions (voyeurism, fetishism, etc.), the equating of ordinary and perverse sexuality, with the concomitant abolition of the distance between the perverse world and that of normal sexual love, is liable to obliterate the specificity of sexual perversion.

It seems to me that, whereas the courtship and love play of ordinary sexual relations do contain some aggressive and exhibitionistic elements, these do not detract from the quality of sadism observed in the perversions. While sexual pleasure and excitation are based on fantasies of union, of penetration, of the use of parts of the body and orifices, as well as on fantasies of possession and aggressive appropriation, the partners' consensual use of the body in the sexual relationship cannot be confused with the characteristic passivity and enslavement of perversion.

As stated earlier, there is no such thing as perversion outside a specific fantasy (which also includes the partner's sensations), a confinement of pleasure within the sadomasochistic monad, a sexuality based on imagination, and an addictive excitatory state.

Kernberg's view goes beyond Freud's intuition concerning the residues of infantile psychosexuality and denies the split-off character of perverse sexuality. The total split between sexuality and love prevents the perverse subject from engaging in other alternatives: his excitation stems from the pleasure of transgressive penetration and from subversion, not from a wish for fusion.

Some of the contemporary literature, as exemplified by Kernberg's contribution, creates a strange impression of blurring in the reader. The non-specific use of terms such as aggression, submission or passivity in different contexts gives rise to confusion in transitions from the phenomenological to the clinical and metapsychological levels. The formula of the polymorphously perverse child is in my view particularly inappropriate for characterizing the devastating outcomes of the sadomasochistic perversion, which has to do not with love but with ecstasy divorced from love.

Aggression in perversion

As stated, in the drive model the child's love for the object is overwhelming, while aggression expresses overweening vitality and the will to conquer. My point is that the primitive Freudian understanding of infantile sexuality as an aggressive, vital drive has an etymological root.[1]

Conversely, in the theory of the life and death drives, Freud distinguishes between relational and destructive aggression.

I should like to point out that the innovation entailed in the theoretical turning point of 1920 and in the 1924 paper, which detaches perversion from primal infantile sexuality, was never fully realized. Closer scrutiny shows that, even after the introduction of the destructive drive into the theoretical model, Freud's thought does not greatly diverge from the first theory, of 1905. In postulating the fusion of the life and death drives, he ultimately attenuates the significance of the destructive action of the death drive when masked by sexual pleasure.

For Freud, sadism and masochism are two excellent examples of the fusion of the two drives (*New Introductory Lectures*, 1933a [1932]): sexual love meets the death drive and forms a mixture in which aggression, destruction and sexuality mingle and temper each other.

The theory of the dualism and fusion of the drives, however, once again involves the mixture of a pair of opposites, the union of and conflict between love and aggression that are characteristic of the component drive ("Instincts and their vicissitudes", 1915c). This may be one reason why a large part of psychoanalytic movement— but not Klein and her followers—failed to develop Freud's intuitions on destructiveness and preferred to retain the model of infantile sexuality.

The fusion of the drives also features in the contemporary analytic literature—in particular, in the work of two authors from very different theoretical schools. The first is Rosen, who writes:

> In general, the high degree of libidinization in perversion serves to bind the increased aggression and hostility, so that physical damage is rarely done to others. Danger occurs when the perversion fails, that is to say there is insufficient libido to contain the aggression. [1979b, p. 54]

The second author is Segal, who states in a more recent contribution:

> Libidinisation is always present as part of fusion of the life and death instincts. But fusion can take many different forms. In healthy development the fusion of the life and death instinct is under the aegis of the life instinct and the deflected death instinct, aggression, is at the service of life. Where the death instinct predominates, the libido is at the service of the death instinct. This is particularly evident in perversions. [1993, p. 59]

However, can a meeting, and mixture, of two antagonistic drives be postulated? If so, would the resulting theoretical construction not make it harder for us to understand the intimate nature of sexual perversion? Does the mitigation of cruelty by sexuality not lead to a "minimalist" view of perversion?

The confusion due to the attenuation effected by the fusion of the drives is compounded by the use of two terms with antithetical meanings, namely aggression and destructiveness.

As already stated several times, sadomasochistic pleasure coincides neither with aggression nor with hate, but with the absence of love—i.e. with indifference. Sadism involves gratuitous oppression because the object's state of consenting passivity allows the cruelty to be planned in a ritual of behaviours thought over in advance. This type of compliant destruction, which thrives on indifference and absence of passion, constitutes the nucleus of perversion.

Whereas aggression and hate may be a violent response to a relational conflict, destructiveness, for its part, is always an anti-relational action; this distinction therefore means that the libidinal and dual-drive models no longer lie on a continuum. In the former, the aggression of the component drive can merge with and be mitigated by infantile sexual love, whereas in the latter destructiveness kills love.

Freud's idea of the fusion of the life and death drives does not mitigate a dangerous fact but actually comes to represent it.

Rosenfeld (1987) rightly points out that, when fusion occurs, it is a successful attempt by the destructive part to colonize the rest of the personality. In this case the violence of the destructive impulse is not tempered but greatly potentiated.

Recent theories

In an attempt to overcome the limits inherent in the psychosexual theory while retaining its main points, Chasseguet-Smirgel (1984, 1992) emphasizes the damaging character of perversion. While her ideas on perversion are undoubtedly well-structured and fascinating, they appear to contradict each other in certain respects.

In her endeavour to keep perversion within the theory of regression as well as within that of the death drive (as a return to the inorganic, undifferentiated state), this author finds herself in difficulties. The postulation of a primitive state in which the pleasure principle coincides with the death drive (Freud's Nirvana principle) leads to a contradiction that cannot be resolved: if life begins where the death drive predominates, how can it possibly develop at all?

The hypothesis of regression to the uterine state raises a number of problems calling for further investigation. Again, regression to the anal world does not explain the high level of destructiveness attained in some perversions; and, finally, not enough emphasis is placed on the quality of the experience of perverse excitation.

Perversion as an act of reparation of the self

Kohut postulates that perverse syndromes can be understood as sexualized outcomes of structural defects. This would explain their particular weakness with respect to the sexual urge: the excess pleasure of the pregenital drive, apart from the need to make good a structural defect, renders perversion irresistible.

In the chapter "A new mode of thinking: narcissism and the psychology of psychosis" of the *Chicago Institute Lectures* (1996), Kohut illustrates his new approach by the case of Patient A, whom he had previously described in *The Analysis of the Self* (1971). This patient's schizophrenic mother had taken pleasure in her child's mental functioning, but had never been able to hug or caress him. A quite serious narcissistic personality disorder accompanied by homosexual perversion had been diagnosed. The perversion took the form of the patient's buying physical-culture magazines which he used for the purposes of masturbation, believing that he could immobilize the man in the photograph with his brain. In his fantasy, the patient bound the man in chains and masturbated him, thereby experiencing an enormous sense of triumph and cohesion. The intensity of the perverse pleasure, which is similar to that of an addiction, therefore stems from sexual pleasure and the triumph of a self suddenly reorganized and reconstituted.

A consistent and systematic follower of Kohut in the field of perversion is Goldberg, who tackled the subject in *The Problem of Perversion* (1994). The title of the Italian version of this book translates as "Perversion and perversions", which gives an idea of the wide range of phenomena covered by the term as well as of an important aspect of the author's treatment, namely a discussion of altered sexual behaviours that cannot readily be defined as perverse in the literal sense of the word.

Goldberg differs from Kernberg in denying the existence of similarities between the aggression of perversion and that present in normal love relations. In his view, the wish to inflict pain does not form part of normal sexuality, but aggression can feature in the expression of the passions without disturbing the joyous pursuit of pleasure.

Rage in general results from failures of the idealized self-object and may be aroused in sexual relations, where grandiosity and the need for fusion with the object are essentially vulnerable.

According to Goldberg, perverse aggression is typically a reaction to the narcissistic wound or loss of control and constitutes an attempt to remedy an injustice (here the author is taking up Stoller's suggestion).

Goldberg seeks to characterize perversion on the basis of specific descriptive parameters. He sees it as a narcissistic disturbance of behaviour distinct from a vertical split, in accordance with Kohut's (1971) position: the self is divided into two parts, each having separate experiences, even if the tendency to preserve unity is maintained. The grandiose self lives separately from the reality self. The essential unity is lost, even though both experiences form part of a single self and are conscious.

A vertical split is thus distinguished from repression, which prevents unconscious material from becoming accessible. However, the problem is not so much of allowing one or other part of the split self to prevail, but of making good the rift—or fault, as it is sometimes called—which is compensated for in the pervert by sexualization. The rift is overcome only by a self-object, the analyst, who is able to do the necessary work on each of the two parts.

Although Goldberg's hypothesis has the merit of presenting perversion as a dynamic phenomenon susceptible to transformation, I find that his attempt to cast new light on perversion is impaired by its recourse to clinical material seemingly selected on the basis of the premises to be demonstrated.

It seems to me that this theory applies mainly to a certain borderline pathology with extensive problems of confusion of personal identity and disturbances of sexual behaviour, but fails to address the specific dynamic of perversion in depth. The concept of a vertical split, too, when applied to disturbances of the self, seems not unlike Freud's idea of a dual reality in perversion, put forward for the first time in "Fetishism" (1927e).

For this reason, Goldberg's book does not, in my view, offer an innovative contribution to the psychoanalytic study of the perverse disorders. It does not appear to go in depth into the problem of sadomasochism, which is completely ignored in the author's examination.

The approach I have described is similar in certain fundamental respects to that of the analysts inspired by Winnicott, such as Masud Khan. For Khan, too, perversion is a heightened instinctuality, in which the drive has to do mainly with excitation. The key element is the anxiety of disintegration, separation or abandonment, which is controlled by the perverse erotization.

In Khan's view, perversion results from damage due to a cumulative trauma, and is at the same time the continuous enactment of an attempt at reparation. He emphasizes the role of the parents, and in particular of the mother, in paving the way for perversion by subtle seductive behaviour.[2]

An obscure point in the theses of both the above authors is the problematical position of perverse sexuality *vis-à-vis* other forms of sexuality. While sexuality is held to perform a cohesive function during development, it is not obvious that this function must necessarily be performed by perverse sexuality. What reason is there to resort to forms of perverse sexuality? Is the contention perhaps that every form of perversion coincides with archaic or autoerotic sexuality?

The excitation and pleasure of normal sexuality could indeed be invoked to support the function of cohesion of a not fully integrated self.

My answer is that the sexualized defences that allay anxiety reflect the level and structure of a personality whose organization is pathological. On each appearance of an intolerable pain or wound, a narcissistic superego is unleashed and drives the subject to compensatory triumph or punitive degradation.

The second paradigm, however, having abandoned the structural hypothesis, cannot describe the process of perverse excitation on the basis of a psychopathological structure, but has to refer solely to anxiety and the cohesive defence.

If fantasy and infantile play are invoked to denote an imaginative world that compensates for the child's impotence, perversion would constitute an exalting experience of impressive performance and a defence against experiences of failure.

Khan's idea that perversion is located within the field of transitional experience, an area that is neither real nor delusional but illusory, seems to offer a better explanation of other forms of perversion, such as exhibitionism, transvestism or fetishism, but fails to account for the specificity of the sadomasochistic perversion, which, unlike the others, has no narcissistic–exhibitionistic components.

The transitional function of the infantile imagination and play is beyond question, but must, in the case of perversion, be correlated with the structure and fantasy that change their meaning. In infantile triumph, domination serves to give pleasure and power, the object being treated benevolently or even with gratitude. In sadomasochism, on the other hand, domination of the other does not serve to achieve fulfilment in performance, as in play: the transitional area is diminished and hence also the object's freedom. Pleasure is concentrated in the wish to exploit a person who must be not only compliant but also "altruistically" prepared to evacuate and obliterate himself for the other. In the forms of perversion in which cruelty predominates, the masochistic object has to be in a state of terrified submission.

Khan holds that the mental state of the perverse subject is similar to that prevailing in dreams and akin to that of a creative artist. He often confuses two levels of primitive experience described by Winnicott, who distinguishes two contrasting modes of fantasying and of having a private world. The first coincides with the transitional space—a primitive, illusional creative world essential to the first experiences of the distinction between me and not-me. The second resembles withdrawal; it absorbs energy and contributes neither to dreaming nor to personal psychic life (Fiamminghi, 1998). Perversion corresponds to this second form of pathological withdrawal into a private, secret space.

I find it hard to conceive of such a similarity. Whereas dream-like states are indeed achieved in perverse performance, the pathways of artists and dreams seem quite unlike those of the perversions. I personally have difficulty in seeing perversion as a defence which has a restructuring function, however temporary. It is surely more likely that the perverse mental state contributes to the progressive destructuring of the ego, sapping its vitality through the addictive dependence on sexual pleasure.

By their emphasis on narcissistic idealization and triumph, the relational hypotheses disregard the excitation of the sadistic parts, which give perversion its particular ecstatic and orgasmic tinge. The intensity of the pleasure should be seen not as facilitating and cohesive but, on the contrary, as a disadvantage.

In conclusion, such an approach is liable to be too consistent with the patient's pathological needs, laying excessive stress on the positive element of development and self-therapy and denying the effect of the subtle and seductive propaganda of perversion.

Perversion as a psychopathological organization

The position of the post-Kleinian analysts is quite remote from the original psychosexual model, perversion being theorized as a pathological organization of the mind in which the balance of the parts of the personality is disturbed. Instead of promoting mental development, sexuality is seen as a product of growth and of the subject's type of internal relations.

In the sadomasochistic perversion, destructiveness, expressed in the excitation of domination and cruelty, becomes sadism. The two components—those of sadism and of libidinal love—are separated; the sexualized bad parts attempt to conquer the good parts without becoming integrated with them, since it is in the nature of the perverse split to make integration and reparation impossible.

This view of course contrasts with Freud's hypothesis of drive fusion as embodied in the theory of the life and death drives.

In the Kleinian perspective, perversion—in contrast to the Freudian contention that it is a deviation from the norm of sexual behaviour or a disturbance of infantile sexuality—is a dynamic situation in which destructiveness predominates and which is merely reinforced by "sexuality".

The nature of the split between destructive and libidinal aspects of the personality distinguishes this theory from other relational approaches: the fundamentally destructive quality of perversion precludes any function of support or repair of damage in the structure of the self.

The post-Kleinian theory of psychopathological structure and the distinction between psychotic and neurotic parts of the personality offer a useful framework for demonstrating the two levels of functioning and their precarious dynamic equilibrium. It also accounts for the process of degradation of the objects of perversion and that of transformation into criminal perversion.

However, the complex dynamics observed in clinical practice show that the post-Kleinian developments have emphasized—or indeed overemphasized—only one of the poles of sadomasochism.

Because it sees perversion as a psychopathological structure, this theory stresses the element of destructive intentionality, under-rating the role of erotization as a defence against persecutory anxiety, as originally highlighted by Klein.

Such an interpretation is appropriate for the structured sexual perversions or perverse characters, but not for borderline pathol-ogies or the cases in which traumatic and persecutory anxiety predominates. The application of this theory, which centres on the force of the destructive drive, presents particular difficulty when it is a matter of assessing the complex relations between perverse symptoms and infantile traumas, abuse-related defences, unconscious identification with the aggressor, or the compulsion to treat parts of the self as they were treated when the subject was a child.

It seems to me that areas of perverse suffering are not satisfactorily accounted for by an excessively strong and powerfully characterized theory such as that of the third paradigm. Again, the special character of pleasure and of the addictive state in perversion are minimized in these theoretical assumptions.

Notwithstanding these limitations, I consider that the line of inquiry developed on the basis of Klein's intuitions has placed perversion in its correct clinical and theoretical framework. In particular, the Kleinian approach has cleared away a source of confusion that has always been present in psychoanalytic constructions—namely, the failure to distinguish between what is infantile, and hence primitive, and what is pathological.

In Freud's *Three Essays* (1905d), the primitive (or infantile) is deemed to coincide with the pathological in the hypothesis that adult perversion consists in a hypertrophic persistence of certain characteristics of infantile sexuality. While this intuition had the merit of contributing to the depathologization of perversion and of allowing it to be understood without social condemnation, it introduced a powerful element of ambiguity. In asserting that "neuroses are [...] the negative of perversions", Freud here contends that neurotic symptoms are the expression of perverse unconscious impulses characteristic of an infantile sexuality. He later demonstrated this by his reconstruction of the infantile history of the Wolf Man (1918b [1914]).

Meltzer (1973) maintains that there is a fundamental distinction between (primitive) polymorphous sexuality and perverse sexuality. Whereas the latter represents a destructive attack on the symbolization of the parental couple, the former belongs to the realm of undifferentiated sensuality.

It follows that Freud, having taken psychosexual monism as his starting point, was unable to distinguish between perversion and primitive polymorphous sexuality. Perversion has to do with the sexual field but, unlike polymorphism, includes a non-sexual destructive aspect (Caper, 1998). For this reason the difference between neurosis and perversion is radical and clear, contrary to what is suggested by Freud's formulation.

The notion that primitive aspects of mind coincide with pathology is also present in the theory of the second paradigm. Albeit not explicitly, Freud's confusion pervades Kohut's theory, which retains the hypothesis (taken from the psychosexual conception) of a stoppage at earlier stages of development, resulting in an alteration in the cohesion of the self. Perversion, too, is seen not specifically as pathology but as involving primitive defensive phases in search of growth. Such a theory seems to suggest that therapy should go back over the stages the patient has never been able to confront for lack of narcissistic reflecting objects. In such cases, the therapeutic setting would be appropriate for making good the primal fault.

In his interesting paper on this subject, Caper (1998) points out that some schools of psychoanalysis identify the primitive with the pathological, on the basis that psychopathological states contain the concreteness, idealization, grandiose fantasies and anxieties observable in the infant psyche. This equation gives rise to the erroneous supposition that pathology is the expression of primitive mental states. This is not, however, the case: the forces at work in the perversions and in psychotic states are destructive and progressively erode the mental capacities, such as the ability to depend on human objects and the possibility of learning from emotional experience, which is the very foundation of psychic health.

Notes

1. Greenacre (1979) notes that the word "aggression" is derived from the Latin *ad-gradi*, meaning "to advance towards"; it only later took on the meaning of an action with hostile intent.
2. This notion resembles Chasseguet-Smirgel's hypothesis of the mother's collusion in the idealization of the pregenital world.

CHAPTER THIRTEEN

Psychoanalytic therapy of the perversions

S o far I have systematically discussed the problems posed by the clinical aspects of perversion, but have had little to say about psychoanalytic therapy with the relevant patients.

I explained at the beginning of this book why analysts have difficulty in presenting clinical accounts of the therapy of perversion in their scientific publications. This limitation, which seriously impedes the exchange of experience among analysts, applies to this study too. However, the presentation of a few psychoanalytic case histories would not only tend to restrict my proposed canvas and its general context, but would also exceed its intended scope. I shall, therefore, confine myself to a few general considerations.

The therapeutic approach to a patient with perversion problems is no different from other forms of therapeutic encounter, except that in these cases the analyst is aware, from the beginning, of the complexity of the clinical situation and of the analysand's problematic position.

In deciding to embark on therapy with a given patient, the analyst formulates reconstructive hypotheses (on the patient's infancy, the objects at his disposal for growth, the causes of blockage in his development, the type of infantile withdrawal that can be identified, and so on), and seeks to understand the level and kind of suffering that can be relieved through the mutative experience of therapy. The historical-reconstructive hypothesis, which serves as our guide for establishing the elements that are present and capable of development, is an indispensable component of the decision to accept a patient in analysis. The psychoanalytic encounter presupposes the existence of two persons who are both involved in a relational situation; this is essential if there is to be any possibility of transformation, and attention must not be confined to the symptom. In this case, however, the symptom remains a territory to be explored. Symptomatic and structural considerations prove to be very useful in cases of perversion.

The perverse symptom often goes unmentioned in the initial interviews, and tends to be less prominent than the patient's general suffering. It is only later that its full significance emerges. When it becomes manifest, its position relative to the balance of the personality as a whole must be determined.

I have attempted in this book to define perversion and place it in its correct clinical context, and it seems to me that this is a basic prerequisite for settling upon a possible therapeutic approach.

Perversion is one of the possible expressions of an alteration of sexual behaviour, but not every behavioural anomaly in the field of sexuality is regarded as perversion. The complemental series of perverse manifestations, which extend, roughly speaking, from secondary, defensive entities to structured pathological organizations, guides the therapeutic approach and determines the course of the treatment.

I shall now attempt a typology of the patients most frequently encountered, with a view to identifying some possible therapeutic pathways.

As stated, the perverse symptom is sometimes localized. For example, it may consist of a set of imagined scenes that accompany intercourse and permit orgasm. Such symptoms are often hidden in the initial interviews and are communicated only in the course of the ensuing psychoanalytic treatment. They tend to arise in a particular type of sensitive and altruistic woman and frequently involve secret fantasies of submission that erotize the encounter with the partner.

In general, an important prognostic factor in psychoanalytic therapy is the extent to which relational and affective experiences have remained intact in the analysand's life. Our guide should be not so much the severity of the symptom as the affective and relational area that can be brought back to life. In the cases considered here, affective life may be impoverished more as a lasting consequence of a traumatic relationship, which prevents the patient from experiencing emotions, than by the presence of a perversion.

Affective relationships and emotional experiences are kept in a state of suspension: as soon as the patient embarks on her analysis, unexplored themes emerge, such as depression, fear of her own vitality, submission to the authority principle, or fear of affective bonds.

In these patients' dreams and associations, the analyst (especially if male) appears as a feared figure that may impose himself and abolish the interiority of the analysand, whereas female figures stand for absent, unreceptive or confusing mothers.

Therapeutic progress involves a delicate transference configuration in which the psychoanalytic space is gradually constituted as a vehicle for relationships, whereby emotional potentialities that have never before been expressed or experienced can be restructured. Particular attention must be devoted to the subjective experience of real trauma, which emerges in analysis with specific characteristics in each patient's history and must be brought out and distinguished from the world of masochistic fantasies. The therapeutic prospects are generally good.

Another common type of pathology encountered in therapy is a narcissistic personality disturbance coupled with impulsive sexual behaviour, often of a homosexual nature. The patients concerned are usually male. As a rule they feel an irresistible impulse to frequent places where sex can be had quickly (cinemas that show pornographic films, public lavatories, certain areas of parks, and the like). This activity is known as cruising.

Although this impulsive behaviour is more frequent in homosexuals, it is also observed in persons with a heterosexual or fluctuating orientation. The impulse arises at particular moments of loneliness when the existential void yawns. Cruising represents a search for excitation, an antidote to the *ennui* of life, a defence against the threatening depressive void. The subjects concerned often have a history of deprivation in infancy, and sustain themselves with excited mental states.

In this type of sexual excitation, the partner must be unknown and the encounter anonymous: what is sought is a body or a penis, not a relationship. Any kind of human relationship, even simple courting, would threaten the excitatory progression, which assumes the character of "turning on" to a drug.

Although such sexual behaviour admittedly has perverse aspects, it cannot be regarded as a perversion proper: the common factor seems to be the dehumanized context of the sexual encounter. The dehumanization not only results from a state of need but is also essential for keeping the excitation alive and inducing orgasm, owing to the predatory nature of the encounter.

Such patients have not developed a capacity to enter into relationships with emotionally significant objects; in other areas too, they function with excited mechanisms that are often manifested in impressive performances on the social stage. Their impulsive sexuality seems to be established as an act that is pleasurable in itself and as a defence against moments of existential void. These subjects' perception of emotion is extremely elementary; lacking introspective capacity, they are driven by impulses of whose origins and dynamics they are unaware.

In all these cases, the psychoanalytic relationship—to the extent that it allows the construction of an internal world—enables the patient gradually to cast off the yoke of impulsive sexualized behaviour, which in almost every respect strongly resembles dependence on drugs.

An important determinant of the therapeutic approach to the group of perversions is the presence of acute fits of anxiety, as in the case of borderline patients who engage in anomalous sexual practices as a protection against psychotic breakdown. The perverse act is episodic, acted out in promiscuous and always variable contexts, and thus differs radically from a true ritualized perversion in which nothing is left to improvization.

Some borderlines with very unstable personal and sexual identities alternate between episodes of sexual acting out and periods when they only have perverse fantasies, which become accessible to analysis.

With such patients, the perverse psychic state must be placed in its correct perspective, so as to give the patient an interpretative key to the type of mental functioning that may be unconsciously dominating his life.

For this purpose it is useful to investigate the first infantile fantasies, when they appeared, and how they were limited or, conversely, gained more and more ground. In all these cases, particular importance attaches to the problem of the confusion of meaning.

Since these patients constantly live in a state of potential confusion that may alter and distort the psychoanalytic relationship, it is important for the analyst to be able to protect the relationship with the patient from sexualized contamination. Excessively "neutral" behaviour or inappropriate interpretations may lead the patient to assume that the therapist is a willing participant. When this occurs, sexual acting out increases, and so does anxiety.

Of course, every therapeutic journey is complex and its course cannot be predicted in detail. During psychoanalytic treatment, the symptom becomes linked to the transference, and certain symptomatic acts betray the kind of object relationship structured by the patient with the analyst. This generally involves anti-emotional defences of domination and control.

I shall merely point out here that many borderline patients in psychoanalysis exhibit "perversions", the understanding of which calls for a differentiated response. With borderline patients, in whom states of perverse excitation are accompanied by simultaneous manifestations of disintegration, the therapeutic prognosis is quite favourable as regards the perverse symptom. In analyses that are going well, it is quite common to observe an attenuation of the perverse excitation and an enrichment of the patient's relational life. Conversely, the unforeseen occurrence or recrudescence of perverse behaviour should give rise to concern about the course of the treatment.

Analysands with a genuine perverse structure—who are in fact seldom encountered—are solitary persons lacking affective relationships, who feel aroused only by the practice of a certain kind of sexuality.

Anxiety is absent in these cases: perversion has become a state of mind coinciding with a vision of the world dominated by the power principle. Although he may cultivate and secretly idealize pleasure, the patient may, deep down, be terrified by the strength of the perversion as he finds himself crossing the boundary into destructive acting out. The fear arises from the risk of losing control and of rashly exposing himself. The anxiety relates to the consequences and not to the behaviour itself.

When the patient's perverse fantasies are nurtured in secret and never acted out, the reason may be terror at the possibility of losing control of his mind and of going mad; in this case it is the consciousness of the disturbance and the struggle between conflicting aspects of the personality that lead to the request for psychotherapy.

The course of the psychoanalytic process is likely to be different in a patient with a structured sexual perversion. Beyond sexual behaviour, perversion corresponds to an internal world devoid of emotions and affective bonds, and the analyst will have his work cut out in his attempt, through the relationship with his patient, to reclaim a cynical, desertified area of the mind.

The subtle destruction of values and compassion typical of the perverse patient tends to induce in the analyst a counter-transference hatred that is seemingly justified by the daily tortures inflicted by the patient on his love objects.

Joseph (1971) describes the constant attack on the analyst's mental stability with its aim of impairing his capacity for understanding. This attack on the analysis is mediated by the creation of a psychoanalytic atmosphere alternating between excitation and frustration. The patient appears to have a finely tuned ability to arouse expectations and then to dash them. The analyst may respond with negative interpretations that lend themselves to inclusion in a sadistic relationship, which the patient experiences as exciting.

In other words, since the patient uses his analysis in a perverse register, the analyst risks reproducing a sadomasochistic cliché with him.

A typical defensive response by the analyst to his own aggressive counter-identification is apathy or boredom, with the concomitant danger of a prolonged impasse in the psychoanalytic process.

The fundamental characteristic of the psychoanalytic treatment of perversion is the gulf between the two protagonists. In so far as the analyst is capable of understanding and listening empathically, the world of perversion appears to him incomprehensible and desperately remote. How can he reach a patient in whom all human values are desertified or subverted?

The innermost core of perverse acting out in analysis is subtle perverse propaganda. The analyst is not immune to it and becomes the target of the prevailing cynicism: psychoanalytic understanding, the symbol of the human relationship, is the butt of prolonged devaluation or is subtly mocked. The patient actively pursues the goal of paradisiacal withdrawal, which he sees as one way of achieving total self-sufficiency and avoiding dependence on a human object.

Many years of analysis are necessary before the patient can escape from the power of the sexualized area and open himself up to the world of emotions and the experience of the positive transference. When this occurs, we realize how the patient has been totally deprived of the experience of emotional relationship, and how the state of withdrawal really has laid waste his mind. The appearance of the human relationship finds him totally unprepared and exposes him to emotional storms that throw him off balance.

To analyse perverse patients, the analyst must constantly maintain an equilibrium, as well as an interest in the world of perversion, its mysteries and singularity; he must adopt a position of simultaneous strength and tolerance, so that the hope of a possible transformation is not thwarted by the wilful cynicism with which the patient will defend his position over long periods.

We are not completely lacking in resources in the therapy of perversion if we succeed in "understanding" it properly. Even in our most seriously ill patients, there are healthy areas with which it is possible to work with good prospects of success. I contend that the failures or crystallizations occurring in our therapies are partly due to a lack of clarity about the incomprehensible and unacceptable aspects of perversion. These threaten our affective world and our stability, giving rise on the one hand to rejection and condemnation and on the other to an edulcorated and spuriously domesticated vision that enfeebles the attentive determination demanded of us by the patient.

CHAPTER FOURTEEN

Evil and pleasure: a psychoanalytic view

Although psychoanalysts are seemingly not well placed to pronounce on the question of evil, since they seldom if ever treat criminal or seriously perverse patients, they nevertheless have the good fortune to investigate, systematically, with due involvement and the appropriate degree of distance, some of the boundary conditions entailed by destructive processes, which I shall now briefly discuss. Over the years, in contact with seriously ill patients in psychoanalytic treatment, I have often come up against silent, self-destructive processes which oppose change and trigger an involutional tendency that cannot easily be halted. The turning point in certain pathologies such as anorexia, drug addiction or psychosis coincides with the moment when the self-destructive impulse ceases to be perceptible to the patient, and the pleasure of physical or emotional self-annihilation takes over from the fear of death.

In this chapter, I should like to present some ideas that took shape in my mind during the composition of this book. These stem from my reflections on and comparison of the various psycho-analytic paradigms and from my clinical experience of "pleasure in evil"—an entity frequently encountered in certain pathological constellations that present themselves to our psychoanalytic observation.

Evil

It is my belief that, in its attempt to remove evil from the objective and moral sphere and to place it instead within the realm of subjectivity, psychoanalytic thought has made a fundamental and original contribution to our understanding of the problems of mental suffering.

The concept of evil, which traditionally involves a personal responsibility and guilt incompatible with the scientific vision of illness, has thus come to constitute an integral part of an explanation of mental pathology. Rather than espousing the prejudice and moral condemnation that have come to surround illness over the centuries, psychoanalysis has permitted significant progress in a field that had been the preserve of philosophical and religious inquiry for hundreds of years.

Two successive conceptions of the link between pleasure and evil can be discerned in the development of this psychoanalytic investigation. In the first, evil is deemed not to merit ethical censure because it is a consequence of the primitive nature of the drives. The second identifies it with destructiveness—the death drive engaged in a struggle with the libidinal part of the personality.

At the meeting of the Vienna Psychoanalytic Society of 9 January 1908, the publisher Hugo Heller read a paper on the history of the devil. Freud ventured an interpretation of his own, according to which the devil was the personification of the unconscious repressed drives and sexual components connected principally with anal erotism. This was the hypothesis presented in "Character and anal erotism" (Freud, 1908b, p. 174), in which, analysing the pleasure of defecation in the anal phase, Freud pointed out that in stories the devil gave his paramours treasures that subsequently turned into excrement: "[...] the devil is certainly nothing else than the personification of the repressed unconscious instinctual life". The devil, as the representative of evil, is purely and simply an expression of the carnal pleasures repressed by the prevailing norms and ethics and combated by the individual himself because he fears them (Di Nola, 1987).

In interpreting neurotic symptoms as stemming from conflicts repressed into the unconscious, Freud soon found himself in the uncomfortable position of having simultaneously to affirm and deny the patient's subjective and personal responsibility for his illness. In the first psychoanalytic cases, he addressed the patient direct and calmed him; whereas on the one hand the neurosis stemmed from the conflicts and aggressive wishes of the primitive infantile drives, at the same time the patient was exonerated from any personal responsibility:

> [...] I pointed out to him that he ought logically to consider himself as in no way responsible for any of these traits in his character; for all of these reprehensible impulses originated from his infancy, and were only derivatives of his infantile character surviving in his unconscious; and he must know that moral responsibility could not be applied to children. It was only by a process of development [...] that a man, with his moral responsibility, grew up out of the sum of his infantile dispositions. He expressed a doubt, however, whether all his evil impulses had originated from that source. [Freud, 1909d, p. 185f.]

Since it is natural for the individual to seek pleasure, it is impossible to consider the situation in terms of full moral responsibility. Furthermore, if therapy is to be possible, the responsibility present unconsciously must be recovered by way of an awareness not catastrophically burdened with guilt. In the primitive psyche, good coincides with what gives pleasure and evil with what causes unpleasure. Genetically, hate precedes love:

> The ego hates, abhors and pursues with intent to destroy all objects which are a source of unpleasurable feeling for it, without taking into account whether they mean a frustration of sexual satisfaction or of the satisfaction of self-preservative needs. [Freud, 1915c, p. 154]

The primitive libido seeks pleasure without any regard to the means of obtaining it. However, man cannot long remain in the position of thinking solely of his own pleasure. At some point, consideration of the common good arises.

Human unhappiness arises out of the fact that, owing to civilization, the individual is compelled to espouse another system, which comes into conflict with the primitive system of the pleasure-ego. This conflict underlies the unconscious sense of guilt. That is why, besides unhappiness, the sense of guilt and illness come into being. Paradoxically, we fall ill because of civilization.

Pleasure

The polarity between pleasure and unpleasure is a constant in Freud's thought. In the *Introductory Lectures on Psycho-Analysis* (1916–1917a [1915–1917], p. 356), he writes: "It seems as though our total mental activity is directed towards achieving pleasure and avoiding unpleasure".

Freud distinguishes a negative pleasure, the relief from pain through the discharge of the drive, from a positive pleasure: "This endeavour has two sides, a positive and a negative aim. It aims, on the one hand, at an absence of pain and unpleasure, and, on the other, at the experiencing of strong feelings of pleasure" (Freud, 1930a [1929], p. 76).

If pleasure corresponds to the fulfilment of a wish, it is satisfaction, the discharge of the wishful tension, and also the cessation of pain and suffering. What causes pain and dissatisfaction are the unsatisfied wishes, which painfully accumulate and must therefore be discharged. For this reason, their satisfaction gives rise to pleasure. Unpleasure that is allayed and becomes pleasure coincides with the drive itself, which tends towards a goal—that is, the goal of pleasure.

In *The Question of Lay Analysis* (1926e, p. 200), Freud writes: "A lowering of the tension of need is felt by our organ of consciousness as pleasurable; an increase of it is soon felt as unpleasure".

According to Sissa (1997), pleasure appears in Freud's oeuvre more often as the lowering of tension—as drive discharge—than as fulfilment and a positive state of pleasure in itself.

This model, which plays down the problem of pleasure as a positive aim, is also applied to sexuality proper—i.e. to the sexual orgasm. Pleasure, according to Freud, is somehow bound up with the diminution, reduction or extinction of the quantity of stimuli active in the psychical apparatus, whereas unpleasure is associated with an increase in this quantity: the pleasure associated with the performance of the sexual act leaves little doubt on this point.

Remaining faithful to the energy-based model of pleasure, Freud took it as the basis of the need to consider the importance of the postponement of satisfaction—that is, the reality principle.

These two entities—the pleasure principle and the reality principle—operate and continue to intersect in the psyche (Freud, 1911b), and pleasure can be obtained only through its own postponement—that is, by taking account of reality.

Although Freud always held to the libidinal model, which pervades his entire oeuvre (so that he even used it to confirm a theory of anxiety based on libidinal frustration or on the non-discharge of libido due to the fear of a fantasized punishment), he nevertheless gradually became aware of the existence of a pleasure connected more with evil, destructiveness or self-destructiveness.

It is no coincidence that *Beyond the Pleasure Principle* (1920g) followed only a year after his second contribution on masochism, "A child is being beaten" (1919e). However, as we know, although Freud became aware after 1920 of the existence of another principle—the death principle—associated with suffering and destruction, he did not apply it consistently to the problem of pleasure, which he continued to see within the dynamic of the libidinal drive.

Even in his discussion of the Nirvana principle, the prototype of the pleasure of self-destruction, Freud remained bound by the energy theory and postulated that this pleasure coincided with the absence of stimuli. He again stressed the idea of negative pleasure, as the absence of suffering: since the libido was a disturbing element, life tended towards the inorganic state and towards death, which coincided with the absence of drives and the search for a state of rest.

Even in his last work, *An Outline of Psycho-Analysis* (1940a [1938]), Freud continued to link pleasure closely to death, while acknowledging that the connection between them remained mysterious:

> The consideration that the pleasure principle demands a reduction, at bottom the extinction perhaps, of the tensions of instinctual needs (that is, *Nirvana*) leads to the still unassessed relations between the pleasure principle and the two primal forces, Eros and the death instinct. [Freud, 1940a [1938], p. 198]

Destructiveness

Through the interaction with Abraham recorded in the correspondence between the two men (Freud & Abraham, 1965a [1907–1926]), Freud discovered the link between mourning, the painful feeling for a lost object, and melancholia (Freud, 1916–1917g [1915]). The core of melancholic pathology lies in the subject's inability to love and in his perception of his own hate. This unconscious perception gives rise to a conscious sense of inadequacy and unworthiness. The admission of guilt excites the pleasure of suffering. The melancholic feels impoverished by his inability to love and his masochistic indulgence in himself. "Knowing" that he is unworthy of love, he tortures both his object and himself. A sadomasochistic vicious circle transforms conscience into an inextinguishable sense of guilt. The superego, that insatiable, hyper-moral persecutor—"a pure culture of the death instinct" (Freud, 1923b, p. 53)—ultimately demands punishment of the guilty party.

The second psychoanalytic theory put forward to explain the transition from evil to pleasure centres on the importance of destructive hate. The concept of evil as unpleasure to be expelled is superseded by that of evil which is incorporated and becomes the engine of pleasure.

For with the overcoming of the psychosexual theory, the opposition between good (pleasure), to be kept inside, and bad (unpleasure), to be thrown out, changes into the conflict between the life drive and the death drive, between love and destructiveness. The importance of the primitive sexual life of the drives is replaced by that of human destructiveness, with the corollary that conscience may be put in the service of love or of hate, as an expression of one or the other.

Evil is therefore destructive hate which also corrupts the conscience.

On the basis of the intuitions of Freud and Abraham, Klein later devised a system of psychoanalytic inquiry that led her to identify the intrinsic forms governing the perception of good and evil. Since destructive acting out gives rise to the sensation of having annihilated the object, the internal world becomes populated with persecutors, which are subsequently perceived as remorse. Hence the need to repair and reconstruct the loved object in a relationship of concern (Klein, 1952).

Klein's concepts of the early recognition of good and bad objects, of good and bad impulses, of the primitive superego, and of the sense of guilt and reparative love, as well as the discovery of psychotic anxieties and mechanisms, bore out the implications of Freud's theory for the unconscious moral sense and the unconscious sense of guilt. The psychoanalytic theory and experience that flowed from Klein's ideas confirm the intuitive basis of natural law and of natural morality—a position that differs radically from all the philosophical arguments put forward as a basis for this theory (Money-Kyrle, 1955).

The sense of right and wrong, of good and bad, develops very early on, laying the foundations for subsequent, more elaborate judgements of good and evil, of rightness and guilt.

The dichotomy of good and evil constitutes the foundation of a method that permits the development of the mind, confers sense on human life and asserts the existence of an order of things: man has an intrinsic code of development consequent upon the acknowledgement of a constructive order that is clearly distinguished from a destructive, confusional demand. It follows from the existence of this order that, whenever adults are unfair or violent in bringing up their children, the result is pathology or suffering in the child.

Klein discusses the possibility of transforming evil: the depressive position, involving the acknowledgement of the subject's own aggression and destructive envy, ultimately makes for love and reparation.

As we know, the Kleinian theory lays extreme emphasis on the dichotomy of good and evil, so that the problem of guilt, as a consequence of innate destructiveness, tends to assume a strongly expiatory significance: healing comes to be seen as substantially coinciding with reparation of the damage done to the object. By placing the love object in a position of ideal goodness, the Kleinian perspective disregards the offences emanating from the object and tends to undervalue defensive, vital hate.

Irreparable evil

But can evil really be mitigated and repaired? And what is evil in the psychoanalytic sense—the evil consequent upon deprivation and abandonment, or the evil generated outside of traumas, which assumes unlimited fascination and power?

The view of Klein's theoretical rival, Anna Freud, too, is that evil is reparable. In the years following the Second World War, she began working with violent and delinquent children abandoned in the wretchedness of that conflict, guided as she was by the idea that only love could, by mixing with it, mitigate hate.

The therapeutic process is sustained by the conception that love (seen as comprehension, sharing and the development of relational and human elements) modifies cruelty, and that evil is reparable.

Until personal responsibility has been consciously elaborated, the unconscious sense of guilt gives rise to behaviour that tends to perpetuate punishment; since evil also generates suffering on account of the harm done to the love object, it can be contained and isolated. Evil may be recalcitrant to any transformation.

Contrary to the hypotheses of Klein and Anna Freud, the problem of the mitigation of evil proves too difficult to solve. In the view of Green (1988), Freud's idea of the opposition between Eros and the destructive drive calls for correction.

Green considers that the destructive drive is pure dissolution, the destruction of meaning—affirming as it does that good is meaningless. Indeed, evil is done through the indifference of the psyche, which finds itself the prisoner of an implacable, mechanical action that can be halted only by the barrage of a countervailing violence.

Cold destructiveness resembles a passionless murder: evil is insensitive to its own and others' pain. Evil is not the opposite of love, but coldness and the absence of love. Transformation is therefore impossible, because any identification with the sufferer is totally blotted out. Destructiveness is first and foremost an attack on the emotions and on the perception of relations between human objects. As Brenman (1985) writes, it gives rise to a specific form of narrow-mindedness, in the absence of which evil could not be perpetuated. For cruelty is maintained by way of radical splits that prevent any understanding.

As I have attempted to show by examination of the sadomaso-chistic perversion, this attack is accompanied by a special form of pleasure, which makes evil preferable to the most powerful good. In my view, evil leads to a form of mental orgasm that enables the subject to act without any awareness or responsibility. That is the main thesis of this book, and the key to understanding the sadomasochistic perversion. The mental pleasure of perverse sexuality is, in the eyes of those who cultivate it, a very special pleasure, much more satisfying than any other kind. It involves an insatiable desire from which any respect for, or understanding of, the other's need and existence is banished. In the specific case of perverse pleasure in its extreme forms, the fascination of absolute, destructive domination of the helpless victim gives rise to a pleasure as stimulating and devastating as a drug.

For this reason, the link between cruelty and mental ecstasy proves to be particularly dangerous. An important factor is that it is not hate-derived evil that affords the maximum of pleasure, but exalting power. When Freud examined sadomasochistic pleasure, he placed it within a paradigm in which mediation of the aggression inherent in sibling rivalry or the Oedipal constellation predomi-nated, and considered perverse pleasure in terms of the psycho-sexual theory ("A child is being beaten", 1919e).

Regression and psychic destruction

Concerning the idealization of the death drive, some psychoanalysts (including Chasseguet-Smirgel, 1986) have described a frantic urge to obtain total satisfaction, to attain the paradise lost where the subject can exist without needs or tensions as the sole inhabitant of the maternal soil.

The wish to return to the intra-uterine state, eliminating all obstacles on the way to the mother's body, seems to constitute what Freud refers to in *Beyond the Pleasure Principle* (1920g) as the death drive—i.e. the anti-libidinal drive.

I have postulated (De Masi, 1996) that the silence that follows the urge towards psychic death and annihilation of the vital defences results from the sexualization of destruction.

Whereas in other mental conditions, such as melancholia, the wish to die is explicit, conscious and a source of suffering, in this mental state which I have described, the auto-sensual pleasure sets the subject on the path towards psychic death; in the race to pleasure, there is no longer any defence or awareness of self-annihilation. Evil becomes an excitant stimulus and a source of pleasure, thereby gaining power over the mind and losing its negative connotation in the eyes of its perpetrator.

Freud knew that extreme states of withdrawal involved a powerful sexual component. One of his letters to Fliess contains the illuminating statement that masturbation is the first and most potent drug. Later, too, in the study of regressed psychotic states, Freud stressed the concept of autoerotism. In the absence of a better definition, this process of withdrawal into sexuality and the body could be termed a state of foetal regression.

By transforming the body into a place of isolation and of internal production of sensuality, the patient discovers how he can fill his perceptual organs with auto-sensuality, putting them out of action without any awareness of the damage done. This gives rise to a "negative" state of pleasure, involving acquiescence and passivity. During the course of this transformation, the patient omnipotently withdraws into his own body, and becomes an "embryo". The experience of transformation in the body is essentially equivalent to a successful act of de-mentalization or de-capitation. Like other psychotic transformations, this process is liable to become an irreversible mutilation of the mind.

Because it entails destruction of the psychical apparatus and of psychic and relational reality, the foetal condition is maintained in parallel with an underlying mental state steeped in pain and anxiety. Inflation of the sense of guilt compels the patient to go on clinging to the auto-sensual island.

I recall a young male patient of mine who suffered terrible anxiety at the thought of being shut up in a coffin, cut off and unable to ask for help. We discovered that the coffin corresponded to auto-sensual withdrawal, a condition that he feared. He was unconsciously aware that the state of foetal withdrawal, which for him was accompanied by the paradisiacal pleasure obtained by the "dismantling" of the sense organs, would subsequently prove to be an anxiety-inducing trap from which it would not be easy to emerge.

Segal (1993) gives the example of a patient of hers who experienced separation as a catastrophic birth and defensively created a situation of psychic withdrawal in which he became a kind of limbless, eyeless and mouth-less embryo. The return to the uterus took the form of a violent and mutilating procedure dictated by the death drive, and not of a benign protective return.

As stated earlier, the minds of seriously ill patients are fascinated by perverse transgression, which, by subverting the organization of the psychic and affective world, gives rise to a sexualized pleasure. In the case of the perversions, psychic regression and pleasure come together to effect an alteration of love relations and of the organizing function of thought and of the affects.

In my view, the psychoanalytic arguments I have outlined help not only to identify a comprehensible link between the problem of evil and that of pleasure, but also to explain the degree and quality of the "evil" at work. I have postulated the existence of various sequences or levels seeking to distinguish themselves from each other: there is a psychically "comprehensible" evil and an evil that is utterly remote from any possibility of comprehension. From the primitive neurotic conflict in the sense of melancholic guilt, these subjects are led by the perverse experience to the state of psychotic disintegration.

Freud (1911b) emphasized the priority of the pleasure principle, which operates even after the consolidation of the capacities for attention, memory and consciousness characteristic of the reality principle. The sexual drive, fantasy, and dreams, as expressions of the pleasure principle, in effect constitute a parallel thought activity, harking back to the primal condition in which withdrawal from the world is achieved at the expense of contact with reality.

The conception I have explored in this book shows that the problem of pleasure is more complex than Freud thought: pleasure does not depend on the defence of the self against the demands of external reality, or on drive discharge. In its production, the destructive mechanisms, directed against the subject's own self or others, seem to be much more efficacious than those involved in the survival of the individual through self-affirmation and satisfaction of the drives.

Destructiveness gives rise to a mental excitation that makes evil pleasurable and irresistible. Hence Sacher-Masoch's specific emphasis on the "over-sensitive" and "over-sensual" character of perverse pleasure. Ecstatic and sensual pleasure is bound up with evil, by which it is fuelled. The good does not give pleasure: it is not visible, but only thinkable. Evil, by contrast, is anchored in the body and is concretely sensual.

REFERENCES

Abraham, K. (1911). Notes on the psycho-analytical investigation and treatment of manic-depressive insanity and allied conditions. In: *Selected Papers on Psycho-Analysis* (pp. 137–156). London: Hogarth, 1927.

Abraham, K. (1916). The first pre-genital stage of the libido. In: *Selected Papers on Psycho-Analysis* (pp. 248–279). London: Hogarth, 1927.

Abraham, K. (1924). A short study of the development of the libido, viewed in the light of mental disorders. In: *Selected Papers on Psycho-Analysis* (pp. 418–501). London: Hogarth, 1927.

Alvarez, A. (1992). *Live Company. Psychoanalytic Psychotherapy with Autistic, Borderline, Deprived and Abused Children.* London and New York: Tavistock, Routledge.

American Psychiatric Association (1994). *Diagnostic and Statistical Manual*, 4th edn. Washington, DC.

Arndt, W. B. (1991). *Gender Disorders and the Paraphilias.* Madison, CT: International Universities Press.

Bach, S. (1994). *The Language of Perversion and the Language of Love.* New York: Aronson.

Balint, M. (1956). Perversions and genitality. In: Lorand & Balint, 1956.

Barale, F., & Ferruta, A. (1997). But is Paris really burning? Uncertainty anxiety and the normal chaos of love. *International Journal of Psycho-Analysis, 78*: 373–378.

Bell, M. R. (1985). *Holy Anorexia*. Chicago: University of Chicago Press.

Bergler, E. (1938). Preliminary phases of the masculine beating fantasy. *Psychoanalytic Quarterly*, 7: 514–536.

Bion, W. (1957). The differentiation of psychotic from non psychotic personalities. *International Journal of Psycho-Analysis*, 38: 266–275.

Brenman, E. (1985). Cruelty and narrowmindness. *International Journal of Psycho-Analysis*, 66: 273–281.

Brenner, C. (1959). The masochistic character: genesis and treatment. *Journal of the American Psychoanalytic Association*, 7: 197–226.

Caper, R. (1998). Psychopathology and primitive mental states. *International Journal of Psycho-Analysis*, 79: 539–551.

Celine, L. F. (1932). *Voyage au bout de la nuit*, Gallimard (Ed.). Paris, 1952.

Chasseguet-Smirgel, J. (1985). *Creativity and Perversion*. London: Free Association Books.

Chasseguet-Smirgel, J. (1986). *Sexuality and Mind*. New York: New York University Press.

Chasseguet-Smirgel, J. (1992). Introduction à la discussion du rapport de Massimo Tomassini: Désidentification primaire, angoisse de séparation et formation de la structure perverse. *Revue Française de Psychanalise*, 56(spécial): 1615–1628.

Coates, S. W., & Moore, S. S. (1997). The complexity of early trauma: representation and transformation. *Psychoanalytic Inquiry*, 17: 286–311.

Coen, S. J. (1981). Sexualization as a predominant mode of defense. *Journal of the American Psychoanalytic Association*, 29: 893–921.

Davies, J. M. (1996). Dissociation, repression, and reality testing in the countertransference: the controversy over memory and false memory in the psychoanalytic treatment of adult survivors of childhood sexual abuse. *Psychoanalytic Dialogues*, 6: 189–218.

Davis, R. H. (1993). Freud's concept of passivity. *Psychological Issues*, Monograph 60. Madison, CT: International Universities Press.

de Laclos, C. (1782). *Les liaisons dangereuses*. Monaco: Editions du Rocher, 1948.

Deleuze, G. (1967). *Présentation de Sacher-Masoch. Le Froid et le Cruel*. Paris: Minuit.

De Martis, D. (1989). La perversione. In: Semi, 1989.

De Masi, F. (1988). Idealizzazione ed erotizzazione nella relazione analitica. *Rivista di Psicoanalisi*, 34: 76–119.

De Masi, F. (1996). Strategie psichiche verso l'autoannientamento. *Rivista di Psicoanalisi*, 42: 549–567.

De M'Uzan, M. (1973). A case of masochistic perversion and an outline of a theory. *International Journal of Psycho-Analysis*, 54: 455–467.

Di Nola, A. (1987). *Il Diavolo*. Rome: Newton Compton.

Dürrenmatt, F. (1998). *Durcheinandertal*. Diogenes, Verlag.

Ellis, H. (1913). Love and pain. In: *Studies in the Psychology of Sex, Volume 2*. New York: Random House, 1936.

Ferenczi, S. (1949). Confusion of tongues between adults and childs. *International Journal of Psycho-Analysis*, 30: 225–230.

Fiamminghi, A. M. (1998). Spazi "privati" della mente nella relazione analitica: una questione teorica e clinica. Read to the Centro Milanese di Psicoanalisi on 7 May 1998.

Foucault, M. (1976). *The History of Sexuality, Volume 1: An Introduction*, R. Hurley (Trans.). Harmondsworth: Penguin, 1981.

Freud, A. (1923). The relation of beating-phantasies to a day-dream. *International Journal of Psycho-Analysis*, 4: 89–102.

Freud, S. (1895d [1893–1895]) (with J. Breuer). *Studies on Hysteria*. *S.E.*, 2: 1–335.

Freud, S. (1905d). *Three Essays on the Theory of Sexuality*. *S.E.*, 7: 125–245.

Freud, S. (1909d). Notes upon a case of obsessional neurosis ("Rat Man"). *S.E.*, 7: 153–249.

Freud, S. (1911a). Psychoanalytic notes upon an autobiographical account of a case of paranoia. *S.E.*, 12: 3–88.

Freud, S. (1911b). Formulations on the two principles of mental functioning. *S.E.*, 12: 215–226.

Freud, S. (1915c). Instincts and their vicissitudes. *S.E.*, 14: 109–140.

Freud, S. (1916–1917a [1915–1917]). *Introductory Lectures on Psycho-Analysis*. *S.E.*, 15: 3–239; 16: 3–496.

Freud, S. (1916–1917g [1915]). Mourning and melancholia. *S.E.*, 14: 237–260.

Freud, S. (1918b [1914]). From the history of an infantile neurosis ("Wolf Man"). *S.E.*, 17: 3–263.

Freud, S. (1919e). "A child is being beaten". *S.E.*, 17: 175–204.

Freud, S. (1919h). The "uncanny". *S.E.*, 17: 217–256.

Freud, S. (1920g). *Beyond the Pleasure Principle*. *S.E.*, 18: 3–64.

Freud, S. (1923b). *The Ego and the Id*. *S.E.*, 19: 3–66.

Freud, S. (1924c). The economic problem of masochism. *S.E.*, 19: 157–170.

Freud, S. (1926e). *The Question of Lay Analysis*. *S.E.*, 20: 179–258.

Freud, S. (1927e). Fetishism. *S.E.*, 21: 149–157.

Freud, S. (1930a [1929]). *Civilization and its Discontents*. *S.E.*, 21: 59–145.

Freud, S. (1931b). Female sexuality. *S.E.*, 21: 223–243.

Freud, S. (1933a [1932]). *New Introductory Lectures on Psycho-Analysis.* *S.E.*, 22: 3–182.

Freud, S. (1940a [1938]). *An Outline of Psycho-Analysis. S.E.*, 23: 141–207.

Freud, S., & Abraham, K. (1965a [1907–1926]). *A Psycho-Analytic Dialogue: The Letters of Sigmund Freud and Karl Abraham 1907–1926*, H. C. Abraham & E. L. Freud (Eds.), B. Marsh & H. C. Abraham (Trans.). London: Hogarth, 1965.

Gillespie, W. H. (1956). The structure and aetiology of sexual perversion. In: Lorand & Balint, 1956.

Glenn, J. (1984). Psychic trauma and masochism. *Journal of the American Psychoanalytic Association*, 32: 357–386.

Glover, E. (1933). The relation of perversion-formation to the development of reality sense. *International Journal of Psycho-Analysis*, 14: 486–504.

Glover, E. (1964). Aggression and sadomasochism. In: *The Pathology and Treatment of Sexual Deviations*. London: Oxford University Press.

Gluckman, C. (1987). Incest in psychic reality. *Journal of Child Psychotherapy*, 13: 109–123.

Goldberg, A. (1994). *The Problem of Perversion*. New Haven, CT: Yale University Press.

Green, A. (1988). Pourquoi le mal? *Nouvelle Revue de Psychanalyse, 38*: 239–261.

Greenacre, P. (1958). Early physical determinants in the development of sense of identity. *Journal of the American Psychoanalytic Association, 6*: 612–627.

Greenacre, P. (1979). Fetishism. In: Rosen, 1979b.

Grossman, W. J. (1986). Notes on masochism: a discussion of the history and development of a psychoanalytic concept. *Psychoanalytic Quarterly, 55*: 379–413.

Grossman, W. J. (1991). Pain, aggression, fantasy, and concepts of sadomasochism. *Psychoanalytic Quarterly, 60*: 22–51.

Harris, T. (1988). *The Silence of the Lambs*. London: Heinemann.

Hartmann, H. (1964). *Essays on Ego Psychology*. New York: International Universities Press.

Imbasciati, A. (1987). Sessualità e piacere come costrutti mentali. *Sessuologia, 1*: 29–40.

Imbasciati, A. (1997). Le origini della dimensione sessuale. Paper read at the Centro Milanese di Psicoanalisi on 13 February 1997.

Joseph, B. (1971). A clinical contribution to the analysis of a perversion. *International Journal of Psycho-Analysis, 52*: 441–449.

Joseph, B. (1982). Addiction to near-death. *International Journal of Psycho-Analysis*, 63: 449–456.

Kagan, J. (1986). *The Nature of the Child.* New York: Basic Books.

Kaplan, L. J. (1991). *Female Perversions: the Temptations of Emma Bovary.* New York: Doubleday.

Kernberg, O. (1991). Sadomasochism, sexual excitement and perversion. *Journal of the American Psychoanalytic Association*, 39: 333–362.

Kernberg, O. (1992). *Aggression in Personality Disorders and Perversions.* New Haven, CT: Yale University Press.

Kernberg, O. (1995). *Love Relations.* New Haven, CT: Yale University Press.

Kerr, J. (1993). *A Most Dangerous Method.* New York: The Analytic Press.

Khan, M. (1979). *Alienation in Perversion.* London: Hogarth.

Klein, M. (1932). *The Psycho-Analysis of Children.* London: Hogarth.

Klein, M. (1952). Envy and gratitude. A study of unconscious sources. In: *The Writings of Melanie Klein, Volume 3.* London: Hogarth.

Kohut, H. (1971). *The Analysis of the Self.* New York: International Universities Press.

Kohut, H. (1977). *The Restoration of the Self.* New York: International Universities Press.

Kohut, H. (1996). *The Chicago Institute Lectures.* Hillsdale, NJ: The Analytic Press.

Krafft-Ebing, R. von (1886/1902). *Psychopathia Sexualis.* New York: Putnam, 1965.

Loewenstein, R. M. (1957). A contribution to the psychoanalytic theory of masochism. *Journal of the American Psychoanalytic Association*, 5: 197–234.

London, J. (1909). *Martin Eden.*

Lorand, S., & Balint, M. (1956). *Perversions: Psychodynamics and Therapy.* New York: Random House.

Mahler, M., Pine, F., & Bergman A. (1975). *The Psychological Birth of the Human Infant.* New York: Basic Books.

Maleson, F. (1984). The multiple meanings of masochism in psycho-analytic discourse. *Journal of the American Psychoanalytic Association*, 32: 325–356.

Marcus, M. (1981). *A Taste for Pain.* London: Souvenir Press.

McDougall, J. (1980). *Plea for a Measure of Abnormality.* New York: International Universities Press.

McDougall, J. (1993). *L'addiction à l'autre: réflexions sur les néosexualités et la sexualité addictive.* Monographie de la Revue Française de Psychanalyse. Les troubles de la sexualité.

McDougall, J. (1995). *The Many Faces of Eros: A Psychoanalytic Exploration of Human Sexuality*. New York: Norton.

McLeod, S. (1981). *The Art of Starvation*. London: Virago.

Meltzer, D. (1966). The relation of anal masturbation to projective identification. *International Journal of Psycho-Analysis*, 47: 335–342.

Meltzer, D. (1973). *Sexual States of Mind*. Perthshire: Clunie Press.

Meltzer, D. (1992). *The Claustrum: An Investigation of Claustrophobic Phenomena*. Perthshire: Clunie Press, for the Roland Harris Educational Trust.

Miller, A. (1980). *For Your Own Good: Hidden Cruelty in Child-Rearing and the Roots of Violence*, H. & H. Hannum (Trans.). London: Faber, 1983.

Mishima, Y. (1960). *Confessions of a Mask*, M. Weatherby (Trans.). London: Paladin, 1988.

Money-Kyrle, R. (1955). Psychoanalysis and ethics. In: *The Collected Papers of Roger Money-Kyrle* (pp. 264–284). Perthshire: Clunie Press, 1978.

Novick, K. K., & Novick, J. (1996). *Fearful Symmetry: the Development and Treatment of Sadomasochism*. Northvale, NJ: Jason Aronson.

Novick, K. K., & Novick, J. (1997). Not for barbarians. An appreciation of Freud's "A Child is being Beaten". In: E. Spector Person (Ed.), *On Freud's "A Child is Being Beaten"* (pp. 31–46). New Haven, CT: Yale University Press.

Panel (1985). Sadomasochism in children. Fall Meeting of the American Psychoanalytic Association, December 22.

Panel (1988). Four sequential panels on sadism and masochism in the psychoanalytic process. Fall Meeting of the American Psychoanalytic Association. New York, December 17, 1988. *Journal of the American Psychoanalytic Association*, 39: 1991.

Parens, H. (1997). The unique pathogenicity of sexual abuse. *Psychoanalytic Inquiry*, 17: 250–266.

Poincaré, J.-H. (1982). The value of science. In: G. B. Halsted (Trans.), *The Foundations of Science*. Washington, DC: University Press of America.

Raimbault, G., & Eliacheff, C. (1989). *Les Indomptables*. Edition Odile Jacob.

Riesenberg Malcolm, R. (1969). The mirror: a perverse sexual fantasy in a woman, seen as a defence against a psychotic breakdown. *British Psycho-Analytical Society Scientific Bulletin*, 37: 1–22.

Rosen, I. (Ed.) (1979b). *Sexual Deviation*, 3rd edn. Oxford: Oxford University Press, 1996.

Rosenfeld, H. A. (1971). A clinical approach to the psychoanalytic theory of the life and death instinct: an investigation into the aggressive aspects of narcissism. *International Journal of Psycho-Analysis*, 52: 169–178.

Rosenfeld, H. A. (1987). On masochism. A theoretical and clinical approach. In: R. A. Glick & D. I. Meyers (Eds.), *Masochism. Current Psychoanalytic Perspectives* (pp. 151–174). Hillsdale, NJ: The Analytic Press.

Sacher-Masoch, L. von (1875). *Venus in Furs*. New York: Sylvan Press, 1947.

Sachs, H. (1923). On the genesis of perversions. *Psychoanalytic Quarterly*, 55: 477–488 (1986).

Sade, D.-A.-F. de (1784). The one hundred and twenty days of Sodom. In: A. Wainhouse & R. Seaver (Comp. & Trans.), *The One Hundred and Twenty Days of Sodom and Other Writings*. London: Arrow, 1991.

Sade, D.-A.-F. de (1795). Philosophy in the bedroom. In: A. Wainhouse & R. Seaver (Comp. & Trans.), *Justine, Philosophy in the Bedroom and Other Writings*. London: Arrow, 1965.

Sandler, J., Holder, A., Dare, C., & Dreher, A. U. (1997). *Freud's Model of the Mind*. London: Karnac.

Schrenk-Notzing, A. von (1895). *The Use of Hypnosis in Psychopathia Sexualis*. New York: Julian Press, 1986.

Segal, H. (1993). On the clinical usefulness of the concept of death instinct. *International Journal of Psycho-Analysis*, 74: 55–63.

Semi, A. A. (Ed.) (1989). *Trattato di psicoanalisi, Volume 2*. Milan: Cortina.

Sissa, G. (1997). *Le plaisir et le mal*. Paris: Odile Jacob.

Smirnoff, V. (1969). The masochistic contract. *International Journal of Psycho-Analysis*, 50: 665–671.

Spitz, R. (1959). *A Genetic Field Theory of Ego Formation*. New York: Pantheon.

Steiner, J. (1982). Perverse relationships between parts of the self: a clinical illustration. *International Journal of Psycho-Analysis*, 63: 241–251.

Steiner, J. (1993). *Psychic Retreats. Pathological Organisations in Psychotic, Neurotic and Borderline Patients*. London: Routledge.

Stoller, R. (1975). *Perversion: The Erotic Form of Hatred*. New York: Pantheon.

Stoller, R. (1985). La perversion et le désir de faire mal. French trans. B. Bost. *Nouvelle Revue de Psychanalyse*, 29: 147–171.

Stoller, R. (1992). *Presentations of Gender*. London: Karnac.

Stolorow, R. D. (1979). Psychosexuality and the representational world. *International Journal of Psycho-Analysis*, 60: 39–45.

Stolorow, R. D., & Grand, H. T. (1973). A partial analysis of a perversion involving bugs. *International Journal of Psycho-Analysis*, 54: 349–350.

Sulloway, F. J. (1979). *Freud, Biologist of the Mind: Beyond the Psychoanalytic Legend*. New York: Basic Books.

Thompson, B. (1994). *Sadomasochism*. London: Cassel.

Thompson, R. F. (1993). *The Brain*, 2nd edn. New York: Freeman.

Winnicott, D. (1945). Primitive emotional development. In: *Through Paediatrics to Psycho-Analysis*. London: Tavistock, 1958.

Young-Bruehl, E. (1988). *Anna Freud. A Biography*. London: Macmillan.

Yourcenar, M. (1980). *Mishima ou la vision du vide*, Gallimard (Ed.), Paris.

Zerbi Schwartz, L. (1998). Trauma nella sessualità. Il trattamento analitico dell'abuso incestuoso infantile. *Rivista di Psicoanalisi*, 44: 527–547.

INDEX

Gluckman, C., 107, 152
Goethe, J. W. von, 91
Goldberg, A., xxii–xxiii, xxv, 63–64,
    83–85, 122–123, 152
Grand, H. T., 115, 156
Granoff, W., 116
Green, xxvi, 144, 152
Greenacre, P., 60, 128, 152
Grossman, W. J., 9, 18, 106, 152
Grunberger, B., 116

Harris, T., xv, xxvi, 152
Hartmann, H., 83, 152
Hate, hatred, xv–xvii, xxi, 21–23, 48, 53,
    69, 97, 101–103, 113, 120, 134, 139,
    142–145
  perversion as the erotic form of, xvi,
    68, 88
  sexuality and, xxiii, 101
Heller, H., 138
Hirschfeld, M., 11
Holder, A., 57, 155
homosexuality, 15, 25, 28–29, 46, 56,
    64–65, 116

idealization, 35, 43, 51, 66, 87, 90, 125,
    128, 145
identification, 22, 27, 46, 62, 69, 71,
    73–74, 81, 95, 105, 108, 117, 127, 134,
    144
identity, 15, 39, 58, 60, 62, 94, 96, 123
  and anatomy, 69, 71
  gender, 46–47, 65, 68–70
  sexual, 4, 46, 29, 71, 106,
imagination, 3, 6, 10, 14, 16, 43, 46,
    70–73, 76–80, 83, 91, 102, 108–109,
    112–114, 118, 124
Imbasciati, A., 71, 152
infancy, 9–11, 38, 60–61, 78, 86–87, 93,
    105–106, 109–110, 112–113, 129, 132,
    139
International Journal of Psycho-Analysis,
    xxviii, 115

Joseph, B., xxi, 48, 83, 98, 107, 134, 152
Jung, C. G., 44

Kagan, J., xxviii, 153
Kaplan, L. J., 18, 153
Kernberg, O. F., xxi, 47, 59–60, 117–118,
    122, 153
Kerr, J., 10, 153
Khan, M. M. R., xxii, 7, 39, 47, 62–63, 84,
    106, 108, 123–125, 153
Klein, M., 47–48, 65–66, 85, 103, 119,
    126–127, 142–144, 153

Kohut, H., xxii, 39, 47, 60–63, 83, 88,
    121–123, 128, 153
Krafft-Ebing, R. Von, 9–11, 13, 16–17, 25,
    56, 91, 153

Lacan, J., 116
libido, 48–49, 54–55, 66, 71–72, 139, 141
  infantile, 6, 46, 117
  neurosis and, 60
  perversion and, 101, 116, 120
Loewenstein, R. M., 17, 153
London, J., 114, 153
Lorand, S., 116, 153
love, xvi–xvii, xix, 3, 14–15, 21–23, 41, 43,
    46, 48–51, 66, 76, 110, 117–118, 121,
    139, 142–144
  absence of, 73, 108, 120, 144
  and perversion, 13–15, 22, 43–44, 47,
    52–53, 55, 58, 64, 73, 78, 87–88, 97,
    99, 103, 110, 115, 118–119, 122,
    126, 134, 142, 147
Löwenfeld, L., 11

Mahler, M. S., 60, 153
Maleson, F., 18, 153
Malraux, A., xxix
Marcus, M., 80, 153
masochism, 6, 9, 10, 16
  and mysticism, 34, 88
  and perverse structure, 40
  and ritualized sexuality, 40
  and separation anxiety, 64
  ascetic, 31–33
  definition of, 16–17
  female/feminine, 18, 25, 40, 56, 110
  infantile, 5, 17, 35, 42–44, 78, 94, 105,
    110, 115, 117
  moral, 25, 55–56
  primary, 34, 55
master/slave, 77, 80–81, 90, 101
masturbation, 10, 13, 26–27, 82, 85, 100,
    117, 122, 146
McDougall, xxii, J., 7, 64–65, 153–154
McLeod, S., 32, 154
melancholia, xi, xxi, 21–23, 142, 145
Meltzer, D., xx–xxi, 7, 19, 48, 66–67,
    85–86, 127, 154
Miller, A., 100–101, 154
Mishima, Y., 41–43, 75, 154
Mitchell, S. A., xxii
Möbius, P. J., 11
Moll, A., 11
Money-Kyrle, R., 143, 154
mother–child, 62, 108
mourning, xi, xiii, 21–22, 142
Murakami, R., 79